AB643

Carole N

Rural Settlement and L

also by Michael Chisholm

Geography and Economics, 1966
(edited with P. Haggett and A. E. Frey) Regional Forecasting, 1971
(edited with G. Manners) Spatial Policy Problems of the British
   Economy, 1971
Research in Human Geography, 1971
(edited) Resources for Britain's Future, 1972
(edited with B. Rodgers) Studies in Human Geography, 1972
(with P. O'Sullivan) Freight Flows and Spatial Aspects of the British
   Economy, 1973
(with J. Oeppen) The Changing Pattern of Employment: Regional
   Specialisation and Industrial Localisation in Britain, 1973
Human Geography: Evolution or Revolution?, 1975
(edited with R. Peel and P. Haggett) Processes in Physical and Human
   Geography: Bristol Essays, 1975

Rural Settlement and Land Use

An Essay in Location

Michael Chisholm

Professor of Geography
University of Cambridge

Hutchinson of London

Hutchinson & Co. (Publishers) Ltd
3 Fitzroy Square, London W1P 6JD

London Melbourne Sydney Auckland
Wellington Johannesburg and agencies
throughout the world

First published 1962
Reprinted 1964, 1965 and 1966
Second edition 1968
Reprinted 1969, 1970, 1972 and 1973
Third edition 1979

Set in Monotype Times New Roman

Printed in Great Britain by The Anchor Press Ltd
and bound by Wm Brendon & Son Ltd
both of Tiptree, Essex

British Library Cataloguing in Publication Data
Chisholm, Michael
　　Rural settlement and land use. – 3rd ed.
　　1. Rural geography
　　I. Title
　　301.35　　GF127
ISBN 0 09 139770 7 cased
　　　　0 09 139771 5 paper

Contents

Figures

Tables

Preface to the third edition

When the first edition of this book appeared in 1962, the so-called quantitative revolution in geography was just beginning to gather momentum. This radical change in the nature of the subject, running parallel with similar changes in other social sciences, has been compounded of two main strands: an interest in theoretical constructs that would allow general statements to be made instead of the description of unique events; and, wherever practicable, a wish to substitute quantitative statements for qualitative ones and to use statistical techniques to provide formal and rigorous tests of hypotheses. With the burgeoning of the literature since 1962 and the progress that has been made in the social sciences generally, it has seemed appropriate to omit most of the original first chapter (the Introduction), which was essentially a defence of the approach adopted in the book. As this apologia no longer seems necessary, the book now starts much more directly with a résumé of the location ideas relating to agriculture expounded by von Thünen in 1826. Though several works incorporating his ideas have been published, and Hall's translation *The Isolated State* appeared in 1966, the summary contained in Chapter 1 remains the most adequate that there is in the English language.

I have kept the original framework of the book, though making a few changes in the order of the argument. I have sought to incorporate new material, to adjust the balance of the text where appropriate and to bring information up to date to the best of my ability. However, since the book was first published, the expansion of the relevant literature has been enormous. Therefore, I fear that much important material cannot be incorporated and it may well be the case that some major studies have been missed.

In my continued reading of published material, I have been impressed by two things in particular. First, although the ideas pertaining to agricultural land-use patterns and settlement locations contained in this book were relatively novel for many readers in the early to mid 1960s, the bulk of the evidence that has subsequently become available can legitimately be interpreted as consistent with von Thünen's ideas at some geographical scale, even if not displaying the clear-cut concentric patterns of land use depicted in the classical diagram (Figure 2, page 20). In many cases, of course, factors other than distance from market are dominant, and in these cases the concentric patterns may be only just evident, or even obliterated.

The second point which has been impressed on me is that, whereas the locational ideas of von Thünen were, for me, a new discovery made in the second half of the 1950s, other authors had in fact already made the same discovery. My own first encounter was on reading Ely and Wehrwein (1940) sometime in the 1950s; they treated von Thünen's ideas in an urban context, which in fact is part of an earlier tradition in urban studies associated with Chicago (see Timms 1971). Although at the time of preparing the first edition I was aware of a number of earlier studies which explicitly referred to the theoretical structure developed by von Thünen, or applied his ideas, there were some of which I was unaware (Mead 1953; Yokeno 1956). Two years before *Rural Settlement and Land Use* first appeared, Schlebecker (1960) introduced agricultural location theory to historians; and, in the same year as the first edition was published, Sautter (1962) issued a wonderfully thorough review of empirical material, albeit without reference to the writing of von Thünen. The following year, Watson's (1963) study of North America was in the bookshops, in which he made explicit reference to the spatial organization of land use in conformity with theory, while in 1964 Galizzi's mainly theoretical work appeared on the market. Thus, to an extent greater than I then realized, the ideas and material contained in this book were beginning to excite the curiosity of scholars in the 1950s and early 1960s.

In preparing the present edition, I have been greatly assisted by Mr G. R. Versey, Department of Geography, University of Cambridge. He drew all the illustrations, assisted with several numerical calculations and also aided my use of libraries by locating references. For this help I am very grateful.

1 Johann Heinrich von Thünen

Of recent years there has been a growing awareness of, and interest in, the problems presented by distances between places on the surface of the earth. Much of this interest has been stimulated by the issues involved in planning a reasonable distribution of employment opportunities in the different parts of Britain and other countries; more recently, there has been a spectacular expansion of interest in economic growth and the problem of getting the 'underdeveloped' countries to the point of 'take-off' into sustained growth. Such matters involve the relative advantages of locations, both in connection with their natural resources and their position relative to other parts of the world. Sociologists, town planners and others have become acutely aware of the social difficulties that arise from a long daily journey to work due to the separation of dwellings and workplaces. One of the objectives in planning is to reduce the amount of circulation necessary for the conduct of the normal business of living. Geographers have for long claimed an interest in the differences which exist between places and there is an increasing awareness among them that many observable variations of phenomena in space are attributable to relative locations rather than to the intrinsic qualities of the individual places. In many other fields of study and endeavour, such as economics and the organization of retail trade, the problems associated with distance and circulation are receiving increased attention; witness of this is given by studies of the influence of distance upon international trading patterns and the care taken in locating large shops and shopping centres.

Distance, then, is the central theme around which this book is written, in an attempt to provide a systematic account of certain features of rural settlement and land use. By developing a systematic study, it has been possible to draw upon a wide range of seemingly unrelated materials to show how these have certain elements in common. In doing this, no claim is made to have elaborated a general theory of universal validity, because the problem of distance is only one among many factors affecting location patterns. However, it is a factor which has its influence everywhere in the world in all location matters, even if at times it is of negligible importance. To obtain a complete understanding of a location problem, the nature of the effects of distance must be appreciated. Though in some cases it may not be very important, it usually has a considerable influence and is often the dominating consideration.

It is at this juncture that the work of location theorists becomes of particular interest, especially that of von Thünen in the context of agricultural land-use patterns and the associated disposition of rural settlements. The logical framework that he developed provides a formal statement of how the agricultural landscape *ought* to be organized, given certain assumptions. His ideas are briefly outlined in the following pages. However, before proceeding it is useful to note some important general points. Whether or not the *exact* pattern shown in Figure 2 ever occurred is not particularly relevant, for as von Thünen himself was at pains to point out his particular findings had no claim to universality. But, as he rightly noted, the analytical method he employed could be applied generally – even, as we shall see, to situations that were beyond his experience at the time he wrote in the nineteenth century. It is the failure to grasp this basic point that has caused many writers to reject von Thünen's ideas as of historical interest only, having no application to modern situations. It is from this initial proposition, that it is the method and not the particular finding which counts, that the character of this chapter derives; an essay in *a priori* reasoning.

Von Thünen published his major work, *The Isolated State*, in 1826, with the avowed aim of discovering the laws which govern the prices of agricultural products and the laws by which price variations are translated into patterns of land use. His was the approach of a practical farming man, for he owned and very successfully operated the estate of Tellow, near Rostock; a point of considerable interest to him was to discover the financially most rewarding system for conducting his enterprise.

His argument started from the premise that the areal distribution of crops and livestock and of types of farming depends upon competition between products and farming systems for the use of any particular plot of land. On any specified piece of land, the enterprise which yields the highest net return wll be conducted and competing enterprises will be relegated to other plots where it is they which yield the highest return. Von Thünen was, then, concerned with two points in particular: (1) the monetary return, over and above the monetary expenses incurred, by different types of agriculture; (2) such net returns pertaining to a unit area of land and not to a unit of product. For example, if a comparison is being made between potatoes and wheat, we will not be concerned with the financial return obtained per tonne of product but with the return which may be expected from a hectare of land in either crop. Thus, at certain locations wheat may be less profitable than potatoes because, although the return per tonne on wheat is higher than on potatoes, the latter yield perhaps three times the weight of crop to a hectare of land. In this case, potatoes will occupy the land.

Economic rent and transfer payments

The actual process of competition for the use of land is more complicated than is suggested in the last paragraph. To analyse the matter von Thünen introduced the concept of Economic Rent, a concept which had been propounded by Ricardo a few years previously (and, indeed, by other authors; see Spiegel 1971). At the time of preparing his first draft, von Thünen was unaware of Ricardo's work, though by the time the first edition of *The Isolated State* was completed he had read Ricardo. Von Thünen arrived at the concept of Economic Rent independently of Ricardo, but the idea, and particularly von Thünen's version of it, had been briefly stated a century and a half earlier by Sir William Petty (Roll 1938). Economic Rent, it must be stated at once, is not the same concept as the term 'rent' in ordinary usage, rent denoting the payment which a tenant makes for the right to occupy a farm or dwelling or other property. Fortunately, we can avoid this confusion by adopting a more modern terminology which nevertheless expresses the ideas which von Thünen expounded.

Imagine a city standing in the centre of a level plain of uniform fertility. This city is the market to which all the agricultural produce is consigned. With uniform fertility we may assume initially that for any given crop the yield is uniform at all locations; this in turn implies that production costs are identical at all sites. However, the farmer has to transport his goods to market, with the result that the net return will vary directly with the transport costs incurred. The further that the farmer is from the market, the greater are these costs of transport and, therefore, the less is the residual difference between the fixed market price and the fixed costs of production. The position is illustrated in Figure 1, which shows the spatial distribution of net revenue for two crops, assuming that production costs do not include any payments for the land used. Clearly, over the radius OY about the city, the net revenue per hectare from potatoes is greater than from wheat, whereas beyond Y the reverse is true. Under these circumstances, and if no other considerations needed to be taken into account, rational (profit-maximizing) farmers would all grow potatoes in the ring defined by the radius OY; at greater distances, all farmers would grow wheat.

The level of prices in the central city has been assumed to be fixed, which is a reasonable assumption so far as the individual producer is concerned. However, the collective decisions envisaged in the previous paragraph may result in an excess or deficit of either (or both) crops. A market imbalance of this nature should be reflected in a change in the absolute, and probably also relative, price levels, to

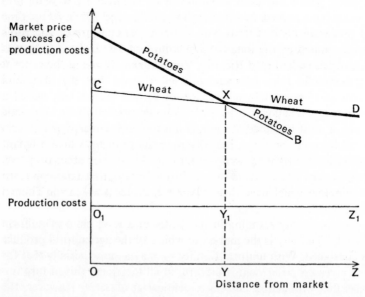

Figure 1 *Revenues for production from one hectare, assuming no cost for the land*

achieve a position in which the supply matches the demand for the commodities at the price prevailing. This in turn will affect the radii of the respective production zones.

Now let us suppose that, instead of many farmers having the use of their land free of charge, they either must buy the farm or rent it. If we now imagine that the production costs shown in Figure 1 include an element of profit ('normal' profits, being the going rate of profit per hectare), then the *maximum* price that could be paid for a hectare of land is the surface depicted boldly in Figure 1, i.e. AXD. The actual price that will be paid will lie somewhere within the range AXD and $O_1 Y_1 Z_1$ whether this is as an annual rental or as a sum for outright purchase representing the capitalization of annual rents. Precisely where within the range the price will actually lie depends on a large number of factors, including the supply (if any) of unused land at the outer margin of cultivation, the number of would-be farmers, institutional arrangements, etc. The payment actually made is known as a transfer payment and represents a share, which may be large or small, of the Economic Rent yielded by cultivation.

Von Thünen developed his ideas in terms of Economic Rent, which he regarded as the surplus produced by the application of labour and other inputs at a given site compared with the return obtainable from the cultivated land the most remote from the central city. This is exactly analogous to the Ricardian concept of Economic Rent based on the soil's inherent fertility; in this case, it is the surplus obtainable by cultivating land of greater fertility than the land of the lowest fertility which is actually used.

The above account is extremely brief and incomplete. Readers who wish to pursue these ideas further should consult one of the standard texts in economics (e.g. Lipsey 1975; Samuelson 1976). Furthermore, the argument has been couched in terms of two crops, either of which is grown to the complete exclusion of the other. In practice, the greater proportion of the world's farming is mixed, depending on the rotation of crops and/or a mixture of cropping and livestock. Therefore, we should think in terms of farming systems rather than single crops.

So far, we have considered only the substitution of products as distance from the market increases. An alternative adjustment is to grow the same crop in a different manner, which will have the effect of altering production costs. Under any particular system of farming, it is possible to vary the level of inputs – such as fertilizers – to a considerable extent. By the 'law' of diminishing returns, each successive increase of inputs yields a smaller increment of production than the last. Under these conditions, if we move towards the market from a distant place, it becomes worth while to intensify production, in so far that savings in transport costs compensate for higher production costs. There will come a point when the advantages to be had from intensifying further the particular system of farming are more than offset by the gain which could be had from an altogether different system. This may be illustrated quite simply. Arable farming with a rotation of cash crops and no livestock is normally an unintensive system of farming compared with an economy based on a rotation of cash crops and grass, the latter being fed to livestock. Both systems can be more or less intensive, but the latter offers much greater scope for raising the output per hectare. In Figure 1, substitute for wheat rotation arable farming without livestock, and for potatoes ley farming with livestock. There is, therefore, a spatial distribution of farming systems as well as of products. Generally – but not exclusively – those systems which have large inputs of manure, labour, etc. are found near the market and the more extensive ones further away. The exceptions are of two kinds: (1) when the production from a hectare is very large despite small inputs, and of small value, as in the case of forestry at the time von Thünen wrote (see page 19); (2) a large quantity of inputs yields a small bulk of valuable end-product, as with butter. The former may be situated near the market, the latter at a considerable remove.

The theoretical argument which has been sketched above refers to only some of the assumptions that are embodied in agricultural location theory. To ensure that a *stable* pattern of agricultural land use will in fact occur, it is necessary to introduce yet further assumptions. In so doing, the discussion quickly becomes very complex. However, the additional assumptions which it is necessary to make are plausible enough and do not suggest that the argument here presented is a highly restricted special case (Dunn 1954; Webber 1972).

The Isolated State

To develop these ideas, von Thünen conceived the idea of a state which had no trade connections with any other nation and was therefore surrounded by an uncultivated wilderness. Within the confines of this imaginary state, the soil was of uniform fertility and there was a single city located centrally, all other habitations being rural. No lines of improved communication crossed the level plain, all goods transport being by horse-drawn carts. Von Thünen then proceeded to examine data collected over a five-year period from his own estate pertaining to the costs of production of various goods, the yields obtained, the costs of transport to market and the ruling market prices. On this basis, he calculated the Economic Rent (net revenue) accruing to each type of land use at various distances from the central city and thereby obtained an ideal distribution of production as a series of concentric circles arranged about the central city. His findings are illustrated in Figure 2. Given the data which were available to him, and the economic/technological conditions of his time, he postulated a radius of 371 km as the outer limit of his Isolated State (Hall 1966).

A point which many writers have seized upon as 'disproving' von Thünen's ideas about agricultural land-use patterns is the position he accorded to forestry as the land-use zone second nearest to the central city. Such a disposition of land uses was not a feature of Europe early in the nineteenth century (Horvath 1967), and certainly does not exist in most developed countries at the present time. However, the postulated existence of this forest ring arises from the application of his principles to the data which were available to him. For forestry, these were for lands managed under a stable re-afforestation programme, whereas in fact Europe, both then and now, relies greatly on the import of timber from virgin forests. The suggested ring of forestry is therefore due to inadequate data pertaining to a non-homogeneous world, rather than to faulty reasoning. Furthermore, there are present-day cases where forests do indeed occupy land near the central city, generally to provide firewood, e.g., Addis Ababa in Ethiopia and Kano in Nigeria.

In the first part of his work, von Thünen presented the model of his 'isolated state' for which he postulated ideal conditions. He then proceeded to use this model as a tool by which he could examine the effects of other variables, to see how they modify the 'ideal' pattern of rural land use. He was keenly aware that there is a host of other factors which all have their influence on the location of agricultural production. The 'isolated state' was never meant to be something that could really exist; indeed, he originally planned to call the work

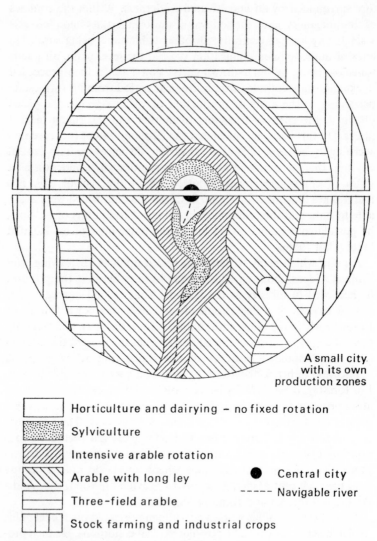

A small city with its own production zones

	Horticulture and dairying – no fixed rotation
	Sylviculture
	Intensive arable rotation
	Arable with long ley
	Three-field arable
	Stock farming and industrial crops

● Central city
----- Navigable river

Figure 2   *Von Thünen's system of land use*

Der Ideale Staat, The Ideal or *Imaginary State*. Once the ideal had been established, deviations from it could be analysed.

There are first of all three points concerned directly with production costs. In his analysis, von Thünen included as a part of production costs the remuneration of the farmer, or that income of the farmer which ensures a 'normal' living wage. In imagination, we may consider this to be the wage which the farmer pays himself for his own labour, equivalent to what he would have had to pay a labourer to do this work. Von Thünen expressed wages in terms of agricultural products, so that as distance from the central city increased, and prices generally tended to decline, monetary wages also fell: but the standard of living remained constant in all parts of the 'isolated state'. This opens up the possibility that the symmetry of his circles will be disturbed if in fact farmers in one part of the country have ideas regarding their just reward that differ from those who inhabit other regions. For example, farmers living near the margin of cultivation may accept a lower standard of living than those nearer the central city; this will depress the cost of production in the marginal areas and enable cultivation to be pushed further into the remoter areas than otherwise would be the case. An example of this is provided by inhabitants of the Appalachian mountains in the United States who have a very meagre standard of living compared with that in most other parts of the country. This can only happen in an economy which is not perfectly adjusted.

The second point in connection with production costs was the observation that many inputs vary in price from one place to another, especially those which originate from the central city. The item which von Thünen particularly had in mind was manure. At that time, urban transport depended upon horses, and milk supply upon urban dairies; together these yielded a plentiful supply of fertilizer which was evacuated to the surrounding countryside. Because of the cost of transport, this manure became progressively more costly as distance from the city increased, until the point was reached at which it ceased to be profitable to purchase manure. This factor, combined with the bulk and perishability of the articles produced, determined the limit of the inner zone of agriculture. However, other kinds of input were included, such as the medical and legal services which all citizens require, the costs of which vary in space.

Third, the soil is not of uniform fertility, and therefore production costs vary substantially. Von Thünen showed that the variability of soil fertility has as big an effect on the location of production as the factor distance. He also noticed the importance of climate in this context, affecting as it does the costs of plant and animal production in various locations. Implicit in this point – and in the others also – is the possibility that where large differences in these factors occur they may be the dominating factor in crop distribution. However, this does not negative his analysis: it merely means that the question of distance which he analysed operates in conjunction with other factors; a *complete* explanation of a particular situation must include this factor of distance, even though in particular cases it be largely obscured by other considerations.

In his initial formulation, von Thünen assumed that the cost of transport was proportional to distance. He later relaxed this assumption somewhat, examining the situation which arises when an improved means of transport is introduced, such as a navigable river or canal, by which transport costs are less than by overland cart. Although the cost of transport along such a route was assumed to be proportional to distance, a journey which used two or more means of transport could involve different costs for the same distance; the actual cost would depend on the proportionate distance travelled by each medium. This line of better communication was assumed to run through the city (see Figure 2). The zones of production expanded along the line of the river, while contracting elsewhere. He also considered the effects of such things as mountain barriers and import duties upon the costs of moving goods. Thus distance must be thought of as economic distance, not merely physical distance; it is the cost incurred and not the distance in so many kilometres which matters.

Von Thünen also abandoned the assumption that there is a single city. He introduced into his analysis a subsidiary city and discussed the manner in which the zones of production are modified. Though he did not press the matter, the idea of a secondary city opens up the possibility of numerous towns of roughly equal importance with production zones which mingle and mutually modify each other. The result, which is common in the real world, is a pattern of extreme complexity, but the difficulty in unravelling the details does not destroy the underlying principle. In Chapter 4 it will be shown that while for practical purposes zoning around individual cities may be rudimentary or indistinguishable, it is relevant to consider aggregations of such cities as single units about which zones of production occur.

Finally, several other factors were explored by von Thünen as modifications to his general scheme, notably the role of trade restrictions, subsidies and taxes. All of these, to a greater or lesser extent, impinge upon the prices of products and hence upon locations of production.

Subsequent workers have taken up the ideas of von Thünen and have sought to introduce improvements. These have not affected the fundamental principles but have attempted to add precision to their formulation and to bring some of the assumptions more nearly into line with reality. We need not concern ourselves with these refinements, for, while important in some respects, they do not add to an understanding of the underlying idea and are not necessary for the arguments developed in the succeeding chapters. The reader who wishes to pursue the matter is referred in particular to Alonso 1964; Benedict 1935; Dunn 1954; Found 1971; Lösch 1954; and Webber 1972.

There is one aspect of von Thünen's work which has received but scant attention. The above account has been couched in terms of the best manner in which to conduct the farm as a whole, given its location, and the pattern of agricultural zones which arises as a consequence. He explicitly observed that exactly the same argument applies to the distribution of cropping, etc., *within* the farm or estate, and devoted much space to an examination of the problem at this scale. The farmer knows the price of any particular product at his farm gate (the market price less the cost of transporting the commodity to market). This, then, is the local price at the farm buildings, which form the centre of operations for the farm. The fields which lie far away from these buildings incur higher costs of operation than do the nearer plots, on account of the greater amount of time spent in travelling back and forth. If the distance is sufficiently great, there will be no profit in cultivating a particular crop on the more distant lands; at a certain distance from the farmstead, the cultivation of that crop will cease. Alternatively, the returns to be had from some other crop will, at a particular distance from the farmstead, become greater: it might be that potatoes are grown on the hither fields and wheat on the further ones. Furthermore, the intensity with which each crop is grown will decline as the distance from the farmstead increases: the farming system will vary from one part of the farm to another. There will thus be a zoning of land use within the farm which repeats certain aspects of the zoning found at larger scales.

Four consequences were noted by von Thünen. First, anyone conducting a farm or estate should look to the costs of cultivating each field and the returns obtained from it and try to arrange the pattern of cropping so that the net return obtained from each field is maximized. Second – a closely related point – for any particular type of farming system there is an optimum areal extent of holding: farm size is therefore closely related to location, this being one of the determinants of farming systems. Third, the distance from the central city at which a particular crop ceases to be grown is affected by the distance within the farm from the farmstead at which it is cultivated. For example, near the central city, wheat may be grown on the furthest fields of the farms. At greater distances from the city, the net return yielded by wheat will be less, but farmers may choose to compensate for this by reducing their production costs. This they could do by growing the wheat nearer the farmstead on fields which, because they are closer, require lower costs of cultivation. In this way, the belt of wheat production could be extended somewhat beyond the limits it would otherwise have. Fourth, there is a consequence important to the question of reorganizing farm holdings. Over much of the world, farms are fragmented, with numerous parcels lying at different distances from the farmsteads. A particular parcel may be far removed from the farmstead from which it is operated, yielding a low or even negative return. If this parcel lies near to some other farmstead, it possesses a higher potential return for this second farmer. If some exchange can be effected which reduces the average distance of the parcels from their respective farmsteads, then the economy of the two farms will be improved and the country as a whole will be slightly better off. This is an important benefit of farm consolidation schemes which springs straight from location principles.

The next chapter develops some further ideas relating to location and shows how the ideas contained in the preceding paragraphs may be expanded in several directions. In Chapter 3 and the following chapters particular points which have been but briefly made in the present chapter are expanded and applied to particular cases.

2 More principles of location

In his exposition of the 'isolated state', von Thünen employed one assumption of which considerable use can be made. The level of prices in the city was assumed to be known, and these prices then formed the datum from which prices in all other parts of the territory were derived. In the 'isolated state', each farmer could know the price he would get for any particular commodity and the cost he would incur in taking it to the market. In effect, he could derive the farmgate price for all goods, and this price formed his own local datum. Each farmer would then select that product or combination of products which yielded the greatest return at his particular location and likewise the most suitable methods of cultivation. But there would be the further problem to allocating each field to its best use, having regard to its location with respect to the farmstead. In fact, within each farm there would be a repetition of some elements of the zoning found in the 'isolated state', centred on the farmstead.

In the 'isolated state', the farmer took his own produce to market, but the above idea is just as valid if we imagine that the farmer sells his produce to a dealer who then acts as a wholesaler in disposing of it; likewise, that the inputs which an operator buys have passed through the hands of a wholesaler and retailer. However long the chain of dealers, the price at any particular point may be regarded as fixed and beyond local control.

An example will make this point clearer. In the absence of trade restrictions, the price of wheat in international trade is effectively set by the price ruling in western Europe, which takes over half the world's imports. At Buenos Aires or Sydney, the price is determined by the European price less the transport costs of shipping the grain. These ports are supplied from elevators in the interior, which in turn are supplied by the local farms, and in each case the price is related to that which can be obtained at the next higher stage of marketing, less the handling costs and dealers' profit margins.

The consequences of this situation may be seen in maps showing variations in the prices received for farm products. Such maps have been compiled for the United States, based on average prices for a number of years, and show very marked regional differences stemming from several causes, among which transport costs are important. For the period 1932–41, the price received by farmers for wheat was over 100 cents a bushel in some eastern areas, falling to below 60 cents in some parts of the mountainous western States (USDA 1953). Some of these data have been used by Warntz (1959), and other examples relevant to the international marketing system may be found in Lösch (1954).

At a local scale, Wanmali (1976) collected data on market prices for some staple foodstuffs for the year 1973–4 in an area near Calcutta. Prices in the weekly market were always higher than in the village market, the difference ranging from 2 per cent for paddy rice to 50 per cent for fish. At the next higher stage in the chain, the terminal (urban) market, the price differential over the weekly market prices ranged between 10 per cent (paddy) and 120 per cent for green coconuts.

In many cases, the above principle is modified by pricing policies which have the effect of averaging prices regionally and destroying the relative advantages conferred by certain locations within the area affected by such a policy. In the United Kingdom, the prices charged for gas and electricity vary between one board and another, but within each area do not differentiate between locations the costs of supplying which vary. The regional variations in prices British farmers receive for liquid milk do not fully reflect differences in the costs of marketing, and the actual farmgate price is nearly uniform over the country.

Such pricing policies do not prevail for all goods; even where they do, there remain certain points in the chain of marketing around which zoning may take place. In the case of milk in Britain, for example, there is no price zoning for the producer until the scale of consideration has been reduced to the individual holding, when it will be in the interest of the farmer not to conduct his dairy enterprise so far from the farmstead that the cost of production swallows up the price he receives.

Scale of consideration

For the purposes of exposition, von Thünen assumed that there was a single city devoid of contact with any other urban centre. But he went on to recognize that in reality there are many centres of consumption (and sources of inputs) with competing spheres of influence, so that the regularity of the zones of production is disturbed. Many subsequent writers have seized upon this to argue that the disturbance becomes so great as to vitiate the principle. The case is that the urban centres are so numerous and so close, the interlocking of production zones so complicated, that in practice they cannot be differentiated, and that in any case transport differences become negligible and other factors assume predominant importance.

Although it is true that in much of Europe and the United States the urban centres are very close together and often run into each other, in other parts of the world this is far from true. Darwin and Melbourne in Australia, Medan and Palembang in Sumatra and Montevideo in Uruguay are sufficiently remote from other major towns to have the essential characteristics of the 'isolated state'. And Brazil has created a brand-new capital in the middle of the Amazonian wilderness: there could be few better examples of isolation from other settlements.

Even a cursory examination will show that it would be vain to seek zones of production around the individual cities of Great Britain: although it is evident that nurserymen are almost always located on the edges of cities, in easy reach of their customers, the production of fruits and vegetables is, apparently perversely, situated in contrasting areas such as Worcestershire and Kent. But if we take a larger scale for consideration, London, Birmingham and Manchester cease to be individual urban centres and become merely parts of a regional market. It then becomes fitting to enquire how agricultural land uses may be disposed about this large market, taking into account not only the British Isles but also all those countries with which we trade. This theme is developed in Chapter 4, where it is shown that zoning of production does occur at this scale.

At the small scale, any individual farm situated in the predominantly urban area has its own problems of spatial organization within its confines; it will remain advantageous to zone production within the holding, irrespective of the external relationships. To this we shall refer in Chapter 3.

The point which has been made in the two preceding paragraphs may be generalized as follows. Though one chooses to regard the market or source of inputs as an infinitely small point, in fact all such 'points' are areas of greater or lesser extent. To regard such an area as a point is only justified if it is small in relation to the total extent under consideration. For a centre of a given size, the area chosen for study must be appropriate; for a given area of enquiry, the size of centre chosen must be suitable.

Location of agriculture and industry

Outwardly, theories of agricultural location based on von Thünen and of industrial location stemming from the work of Weber (1929) are radically different. The best-known feature of the former is the rings of land use that surround the central city, whereas the hallmark of the latter is the optimum location for a single industrial plant. In the initial von Thünen model, the problem is to determine the optimum *production* for a farm the location of which is given. In the Weberian case the problem is reversed; given the type of production, what is the optimum *location*? There is no difference in principle between those two approaches: it is merely that a different factor is allowed to vary. In both models it is assumed that the following are known: location of the destination of the produce; location of the sources of inputs (coal or manure, etc.); and the scale of the enterprise being undertaken (though later writers have allowed for scale economies). In addition, in the von Thünen case the location of production is known, and the question is to determine the best form of activity; in the Weberian case, the problem is reversed. However, as Hamilton (1974) has noted, the position may arise in the manufacturing sector in which an entrepreneur occupies a location and must choose what to manufacture.

Both the agricultural and industrial cases are problems of optimization, i.e. to find the 'best' solution given the various assumptions made. In effect, they are special cases of the general case embodied in micro-economic theory of the firm, in which the rational decision-maker maximizes his profits. In the industrial problem formulated by Weber, there may be only one firm and therefore a unique location will be chosen. However, Weber himself envisaged that there may be cases in which several firms agglomerate together into towns. The agricultural case involves a very large number of firms (farms). As envisaged by von Thünen, all of the farmer entrepreneurs are faced with the same objective external world, all are rational profit-maximizers and therefore neighbours all come to the same decision, except at the boundary between two farming systems. Hence arise the zones of production, equivalent to the urban agglomeration of manufacturing activities.

The assumption of fully rational, profit-maximizing behaviour is of course a very strong one. At the very least, it implies a formidable amount of knowledge on the part of farmers. Under stable technical and environmental conditions, it is reasonable to suppose that, as one generation succeeds another, the farming community will adapt its practice and settlement system to achieve, if not the maximum feasible income, then at least the best strategy for survival (Schultz 1964; Lipton 1968). To the extent that information is lacking and/or decisions are less than fully rational, the patterns manifest in the real world will diverge from those which theoretical considerations would lead one to expect (Pred 1967 and 1969). Such divergence does not negate the value of the theory but suggests avenues for further enquiry. If we allow that all farmers seek to maximize their income we are faced with the question: over what period of time? In the more arid midwest of the United States, for example, the maximum short-term income may be obtained by the monoculture of wheat, at the expense of a deterioration of the soil which ultimately will put an end to all cropping. For a long-period maximum income from the same land a mixed system of grazing and infrequent ploughing may be necessary. Consequently, the pursuit of maximum income may lead to radically different systems on two adjacent farms, the contrast arising from the different time periods envisaged by the two farmers. To understand these differing valuations of future time, one must embark on the difficult task of unravelling people's perceptions of the environment. This is a field of enquiry that has burgeoned since White (1945) published his dissertation on flood hazards, Gould (1963) formulated man's activities as a game with nature and Wolpert (1964) showed how the actual returns from farming in a part of Sweden compared with the potential output. The reader who wishes to pursue this matter has a wide choice of literature to which to turn (e.g. Brookfield 1969; Prince 1971; Downs and Stea 1973; Gould and White 1974; Tuan 1977).

Despite the reservations mentioned above, the available empirical material suggests that farmers all over the world get sufficiently close to the 'rational' pattern of cultivation sufficiently often for the ideas expounded by von Thünen to be regarded as providing a good explanation of what actually happens.

Other explanations

Von Thünen couched his argument in terms of a static equilibrium, i.e. a stable situation that could be expected to occur given the assumptions made. This formulation implies that no new impulse is introduced into the system. The fact that such new impulses are continuously being generated does not invalidate the static equilibrium approach, though it does create difficulties in two separate ways. In the first place, if technical and economic conditions are indeed changing, then in making assumptions (about yields, production costs, transport costs, prices, etc.), it may be difficult to know what values are the realistic ones to accept in order to apply theory in any particular case. There is, therefore, an important logical problem if one wishes to compare the patterns observed in the real world with the patterns that might be expected, owing to the difficulty of specifying exactly what is the 'expected' position. However, as will become apparent in the chapters that follow, this problem is not too serious in practice.

In some respects, it is the second effect of technical and economic change that is both harder to cope with and more interesting. Put generally, the effect is to create conditions in which concentric zoning of land uses may occur for reasons that differ from those specified by von Thünen. In particular, some dynamic processes lead to the inversion of the generally expected arrangement of less intensive land uses at greater distances from the central city (Falque 1973). Sinclair (1967) was one of the first writers to draw attention to a relatively novel phenomenon around many expanding cities. With the spread of residential and other development onto agricultural land, farmers recognize the possibility of their property fetching a high price and adjust their farming practices so that a sale can be made at short notice. Likewise, property speculators buy farms and then rent the land on short-term leases. As a result, labour and other inputs are reduced and the land deteriorates, while the farming system changes from intensive modes of production to extensive ones and land may even go out of use entirely. Sinclair provided a certain amount of empirical evidence to show that this inversion process does actually happen, evidence confirmed for the United States by Clawson (1971), and Boal (1970) for the area around Belfast in Ulster, where in the 1950s between 30 and 40 per cent of the land was rented under leases of about one year and was used mainly for stock fattening.

Since the Second World War, part-time farming has become much more important. Many farms in the vicinity of big towns have been bought up by commuting city workers, who live in the farm-house and cultivate some or all of the property (the remainder is either sold or leased). In some cases, the part-time farming may be associated with a second home, rather than the primary residence. Gottmann (1961) noted that in 1954 in the heavily urbanized north-east of the United States, part-time farmers accounted for between one-fifth and one-third of the farm area of states such as Massachusetts, Rhode Island and Connecticut, although making a negligible contribution to output. That something rather similar has happened in Britain is indicated by a survey of the area around Slough, on the western edge of the London conurbation. Of 332 farms surveyed, almost one-half were part-time, operated on a low-intensity basis (ADAS 1973). Although these cases represent the more extreme development of part-time farming, approximately 15 per cent of all farmers in the original six member countries of the EEC were operating part-time in 1966–7 (EEC 1977).

For a balanced review of the above considerations, the reader is referred to Munton (1974). Yet another process is operating in developed countries to modify the pattern of rural land use at considerable distances from major urban centres, namely, the ownership of second homes. This modern phenomenon is most evident in Sweden, where by 1967 about one household in seven had a second residence in the country (Ödmann and Dahlberg 1970). Although the majority of second homes are relatively close, distances of up to 100–200 km are considered acceptable.

When a new crop is introduced into a traditional agricultural economy, a new zoning of crops may occur around the settlement that has little to do with the principles of labour economy. Lockwood (1971) reports that in Samoan villages coconuts were planted as a cash crop, especially in the period 1880 to 1920. Coconuts require relatively little labour and in many societies are relegated to the more distant lands. In the villages studied by Lockwood, the pattern was in fact reversed, with the coconuts occupying land near the settlement that formerly was planted to food crops. No doubt questions of novelty and social status were responsible for this inversion of the normal land-use pattern (see also Morgan 1973).

Finally, a very low intensity of land use may be apparent around permanent settlements where long-continued cultivation has led to serious impoverishment and even soil erosion. The city of Ibadan, Nigeria, has approximately one million inhabitants. Since the 1930s, within a radius of about 8 km of the city centre, the traditional bush-fallow agriculture had been unable to sustain output and cassava and cocoyams are the only crops that will grow; elsewhere, useless grasses have invaded the impoverished soils and gully erosion is rampant (Oluwasanmi 1967).

The East Africa Royal Commission (1955) found that, under conditions of head porterage, the cultivation of maize near coastal villages had resulted in serious damage, while bush remained un-cleared further away on account of high transport costs. Indeed, Jackson (1972) cites evidence suggesting that low intensity of land use near settlements, arising from soil exhaustion, is a common phenomenon in Africa, as around Kano, Kampala and elsewhere. The same problem has been reported elsewhere, Singapore and St Vincent being two cities in question.

The previous paragraphs have indicated that more than one process may be operating which tends to reverse or substantially modify the sequence of land uses predicted by the theoretical approach of von Thünen. By the same token, there may also be numerous other processes which result in patterns similar to those predicted by theory. Thus, the reader is asked to note that while the empirical evidence cited in the following chapters is consistent with the model developed by von Thünen, there may be alternative constructions of equal plausibility.

The last few paragraphs are intended to warn the reader against seeing in the material which follows a degree of accuracy greater than in fact exists and to obviate the need for repeated qualifications throughout the following chapters. However, it will become abundantly clear that despite these qualifications there are striking regularities in location patterns throughout the world, conforming to the theoretical concepts which have been expounded.

3   The farm and the village

In this chapter, attention will be devoted exclusively to the farm, hamlet and village. Because the order of distance involved is the same in all three cases, the mode of argument is identical, or nearly identical. Furthermore, in many cases the pattern of land use around a hamlet or village is but the sum of patterns subsisting on individual holdings which are fragmented, the plots being scattered all over the territory of the hamlet or village.

For the purpose of this chapter, we will regard the position of the farmstead as given and known: likewise, the position of the hamlet or village, since this comprises a large number of farmsteads. We may then envisage the farm in the following terms:

(1) The farmstead, or the farm-house and farm buildings, is the point of origin for all the inputs which have to be applied to the land of the farm. There the farmer and his family live, leaving the farmstead each morning for the fields and returning to it in the evening and possibly at intervals during the day. Likewise, the manure accumulates in the yard or stables and the artificial fertilizers are stored in the barn, and these and everything else which is applied to the land must be taken thence to the fields.

(2) The farmstead is also the point to which all the produce of the farm is brought, either for consumption there or onward shipment to the local dealer or market. The farmstead may quite justly be regarded as the first point in the chain of marketing, in the sense of being a collecting and clearing centre, though actual market transactions do not normally take place there.

Exactly the same model may be envisaged for the hamlet or village where the dwellings of those who cultivate the surrounding land are collected: all inputs emanate thence, all produce is consigned thither.

This is an over-simplified account which omits to consider some

B

exceptions. For example, some produce may be shipped straight from the fields to a local factory or dealer and so never pass through the farmstead or village; or some workers may live away from the farmer's dwelling, even in another village, and be able to proceed direct to the scene of operations for the day without recourse to the farmstead for instructions. However, these minor modifications do not in any essential manner impair the utility of considering the farmstead or hamlet or village as the 'isolated state' that von Thünen conceived, stripped of the complications that in reality arise from competing or overlapping market areas.

In considering the manner in which a farm is operated, it will immediately be apparent that distance is important in relation to the movement both of goods and persons, and furthermore that the former requires the latter. Discounting recent experimental work on remote-controlled tractors, the shifting of any commodity or implement implies also the translocation of at least one person. Similarly, a change in job will usually involve a change in situation. Hence, all movement on a farm may be expressed in terms of man-hours, supplemented by tractor and draught animal-hours. Strictly speaking, it is not time as such that matters but the value of the time, measured either as the wages paid to the workers or as production foregone (the opportunity cost). Unfortunately, it is an extremely laborious matter to collect data on the spatial pattern of labour inputs and travel time within a farm or village territory. Even if this kind of information were readily available, there would be serious problems in converting data on time into data on costs. In practice, therefore, it is generally necessary to couch the argument in terms of physical distance (kilometres) rather than in terms of either time or cost. One of the earliest, and still one of the very few, maps showing isochrones for farm operations is that compiled by Müller-Wille (1936) for carting manure to the fields.

If a farmer behaves in a rational fashion, he will be interested in conducting his holding so that the cost of the last unit of labour bestowed equals the value of the additional produce which will result from it. If in fact the cost of this last (or marginal) amount of labour exceeds the value of the marginal return, then he will tend to curtail his operations, and vice versa. For this overall situation to obtain, the same must be true of each field or parcel: if it did not, then a simple transfer of effort from one field, where the cost of the marginal dose of labour exceeded the value of the return, to another where the reverse situation prevailed, would enable the farmer to increase his product without any increment in the cost of labour. Now, the total time involved in cultivating a field for an additional hour rises the further removed it is, since the time consumed in travelling must be added in. It follows, therefore, that the return from this last hour of actual work must be greater on the more distant plot than on the nearer, to compensate for the time spent in travelling. This will result in a lesser degree of intensity of farming at the greater remove, through the operation of the 'law' of diminishing returns. It is an observed fact that in agriculture each successive dose of inputs – say hours of work – tends to yield a smaller and smaller return as the total amount of inputs – the total number of hours worked – rises. Hence, the farmer will desist at a point earlier on the curve of diminishing returns the more each actual hour of work applied to the land costs; which is to say, the further away is the field. The point has equal force whether or not the farmer hires any labour, the argument applying to both wage labour and family work.

Therefore, the first matter to which we must turn is an examination of the available evidence regarding actual distances between farmsteads and cultivated land.

Distances involved

At the present time, perhaps the most widespread single cause of large distances is the fragmentation of holdings and this phenomenon has received a good deal of attention. It is easy to cite extreme cases where plots may be 10 or even 20 kilometres distant from the farmstead; there is much less information available on the normal or common magnitudes involved. Even in Europe, which in *circa* 1960 had a greater degree of fragmentation than any other continent, with approximately 6.7 plots per holding (F A O 1971), the information is limited. Prior to the post-war programmes of consolidation it was estimated that in Finland the average distance of the fields from the dwelling was between 1.0 and 1.1 kilometre (Pihkala and Suomela 1952); in the Netherlands, the average was 1.1 kilometre, varying from 0.8 in Utrecht to 1.4 in Noord-Brabant (Hofstee 1957). Using a rather indirect method of estimation, based on median village sizes and average number of plots per person, Dovring (1965a) calculated the regional variation in theoretical average distance to plots to be (in kilometres):

Belgium	0.3–1.0	West Germany	0.3–2.0
Netherlands	0.3–1.0	Bulgaria	2.0
Switzerland	0.3–1.0	Romania	0.7–2.5
France	0.3–2.0	Spain	0.3–6.0

These averages conceal wide regional variations within the respective countries, which in turn reflect, at least in part, substantial regional differences in the amount of fragmentation (Fennell 1977).

Asia is the continent with the second greatest problem of fragmentation, having 4.0 plots per holding in *circa* 1960. In his mammoth survey of Chinese land use Buck (1937) found that in a sample of nearly 17,000 farms the average distance between farmstead and field was 0.6 kilometre, ranging from 0.3 in the Szechwan Rice Region to 1.0 in the Spring Wheat Region. The average distance to the furthest parcels was 1.1 kilometre for the country as a whole, varying from 0.5 to 1.8 as the respective extremes for the two named regions. A very similar picture emerges in the case of Pakistan, where a survey of forty villages in the Punjab showed that almost half of the 356 holdings were fragmented, and that on these the average distances of the parcels from the main plots were as shown in Table 1.

Table 1 *Pakistan: average distance of plots from the main plot*

Distance (km)	Number of holdings	
	actual	per cent
less than 0.8	70	40.2
1.0–1.6	63	36.2
1.8–3.2	30	17.3
over 3.2	11	6.3
Total	174	100.0

Source: Khan 1955

Although fragmentation is a less serious problem in other continents, similar distances do occur, certainly in Jamaica (Edwards 1961) and Tanzania (Hirst 1970). Hirst found that for a sample of 5000 households, 50 per cent were less than 2.5 kilometres from their land on average, and 83 per cent under 4 kilometres. Interestingly enough, the problem has now appeared in the United States, a country which used to be characterized by farms laid out in a single block (Smith 1975; Sublett 1975). Faced with pressure on their profits and technological changes, farmers have felt the need to enlarge their holdings. This they do either by renting or buying land, as it becomes available on the market. As a consequence, the relatively minor fragmentation which can be traced to early colonization has changed dramatically in the post-war period. Smith cites cases in which the most distant land is 40 kilometres from the base of operations, a distance confirmed by Sublett. The latter carefully surveyed three counties on the outer fringes of the Chicago metropolitan area, finding that whereas the mean distance to outlying land for farmers with non-contiguous plots was of the order 2.7–3.5 kilometres in 1939, the equivalent range in 1969 was 13–18 kilometres. In the special case of cotton production, the acreage that may be planted is controlled; therefore if a farmer is to enlarge his scale of cotton output he must acquire other properties and thereby their acreage quotas. Thus, in the Piedmont region of the USA, cotton fields are managed over a radius of 15–20 kilometres around the home farm (Prunty and Aiken 1972). In the American context, it is possible to farm land at such distances only by using tractors and motor cars; even so, a distance of 40 kilometres implies a one-way journey of 60 minutes by tractor.

Another reason for the existence of great distances is a rather peculiar and much less widespread form of holding, in which the properties are very narrow and grossly elongated. Apparently originating with the Germanic peoples about AD 1000 (Eidt 1971; Jordan 1974), it seems likely that these *Hufenflur* settlements represent the progressive clearance of forest or swamp from either an initial road or the high ground of a levee, along which the farmsteads were located. Holdings exceeding 3.0 kilometres in length have been reported from the Netherlands (Bijhouwer 1949). Although there is some doubt whether the system was transferred to the New World by settlers and colonial administrators or evolved independently (Carlson 1975), there is no doubt that it occurs very widely in the Americas. Harris (1966) records the system along the St Lawrence River, and in Brazil holdings exceed 3.0 kilometres in length (Meynier 1958); the astonishing figure of 24 kilometres has been recorded in Texas (Jordan 1974). This New World occurrence of *Hufenflur* settlements appears to be associated with progressive clearance of virgin lands from a roadside or river frontage, thus being comparable to the medieval system in Europe.

Distance may be considerable where the land of a village is farmed as a unit, in common, a system widespread in the days of the open fields, but now of small importance, except in Eastern Europe and the USSR where collective and co-operative farms exist. Finally, where there are large estates worked from a single centre, such as the European-established plantations found in many tropical and subtropical regions, distances may again be considerable.

In the foregoing discussion, it has been assumed that distance can be measured as the crow-flight distance from the parcel to the farmstead. In practice, most plots have only one or two points of access and the route from these to the farmstead may be devious. Normally, therefore, the actual distances which have to be traversed are greater than indicated. In some cases this is offset where the fields are very large, as on Russian collective farms. For certain operations, such as ploughing, it does not matter if the arable area extends to a great distance, for the tractor is performing useful and necessary work while it proceeds to the further limits drawing the plough behind.

In relation to the fact that the average distance to the cultivated land is commonly of the order of one kilometre or more and very frequently rises to three or four, it is pertinent to observe that the weight of goods moved in the course of one year is notable, contributing appreciably to the costs which distance imposes. On three French farms, practising a mixed system of cultivation, the figures for all goods moved in one year (including produce and fertilizer) were (Piel-Desruisseaux n.d.):

Farm	Tonnes per hectare
(1) Gâtinais, 25 hectares	15.4
(2) Aube, 144 hectares	16.5
(3) Seine et Oise, 145 hectares	18.0

That these figures are likely to be representative of much of western Europe is indicated by the data available for the United Kingdom pertaining to the quantities of various agricultural items produced and the purchases by farmers of lime, fertilizers and feeding-stuffs. From these it can be estimated that the minimum quantity of all commodities handled per hectare per annum on an ordinary British farm is 7 metric tons and that the average weight is likely to be at least 10. This is an order of magnitude that in Africa is matched only in rather special circumstances. One such case is the exceptionally intensive farming on the island of Ukara, Lake Victoria; the high intensity of farming is dependent upon very large inputs of manure which, when added to the volume of produce, results in some 7 to 15 tonnes of material per hectare to be transported each year, most of it head-loaded (Ludwig 1968). On the other hand, in regions of extensive cultivation, especially the semi-arid regions of the world, the weight handled annually is considerably less. The lower limit is probably found with shifting cultivators who do not manure their land; yields in the order of one to two tonnes per hectare seem to be common (Clark and Haswell 1970).

Table 2 *Agricultural time spent travelling to and from the farm plots as a percentage of agricultural labour time*

Gambia (Jackson 1972)	10–12
Uganda, Lango District (Jackson 1972)	15
Southern Ghana, cocoa growers (Okali 1975)	15
Zaire, Uélé (de Smet 1972)	18
Uganda, SW and NW (Jackson 1972)	over 25
Southern Ghana, lime growers (Wagenbuur 1972)	
includes preparation time males	27
females	33
SE Nigeria, oil palm growers (Martin 1956)	33
Nicaragua, east coast (Nietschmann 1973)	
coconut grove, 4.8 km	28
subsistence crops, new plantation, 4.8 km	29
subsistence crops, one year plantation, 4.8 km	33
rice plantation, 27.4 km	51

As a result of the distances involved and the quantities of commodities to be moved, the proportion of all working time spent in movement is about one-third on British farms (*The Times*, 24 November 1962); in the Netherlands, over half the working hours of horses and tractors may be devoted to the movement of produce and materials (Coolman and Willems 1960). Studies in various parts of Africa show that between one-tenth and one-third of agricultural time is spent travelling to and fro (Table 2). It seems likely that the order of magnitude is similar in much of the rest of the world and it is therefore hardly surprising that farmers do in fact adjust their activities, including the spatial pattern of their operations, with the intent to economize effort.

Adjustments to distance

This section starts with a review of evidence showing that the amount of labour actually applied to the land does decrease with distance from the farmstead. Thereafter, attention turns to the consequential effects upon gross and net output. In the light of the quantitative evidence thus presented it is then possible to interpret the large mass of more descriptive material that is available.

Workstudy observation by Visser (1950) showed that the amount of time actually applied to the land (i.e. travel time excluded) followed the pattern shown in Table 3. The more recent study by Blaikie (1971) for sample villages in India, although not based on workstudy measurements in quite the same way as Visser's, nevertheless shows that in at least one case of dry farming the actual labour input drops by between one-quarter and one-third within 2 kilometres of the village (see also Figure 3, page 46).

Table 3 *Netherlands: man-hours per annum per hectare actually worked on plots of over 15 hectares*

Distance from farmstead (km)	Grassland plots	Arable plots
0.5	220	400
1.0	210	360
2.0	180	300
3.0	160	240
4.0	130	190
5.0	110	150

Source: Visser 1950

Given the evident curtailment of effort at greater distances, we would expect gross output also to decline, and probably also net output. That this is indeed the case has been attested in a number of studies.

A detailed survey was carried out by Wiiala (1948) on a single parish in Finland, with the object of measuring the benefits to be obtained from the consolidation of the holdings. From the accounts kept by the farmers, he was able to measure the effect of distance upon the level of gross and net production, as measured in money terms. This he did by computing the average distance of the fields from the farmstead for each farm and the average return (gross and net) per hectare. He found that as the average distance increased, the per hectare returns declined, and he was able to obtain an algebraic relationship from which the figures in Table 4 have been computed. The net produce declines much more rapidly than the gross output, a situation which arises from the fact that the level of costs actually incurred diminishes less swiftly than the level of gross produce. His figures indicate that at an average distance of but 1 kilometre the gross return has fallen by 16 per cent and the net return by 44 per cent: at 2 kilometres the net return per hectare is very small. Much the same result was obtained in another study of a Finnish community conducted by Virri (1946), in which he found a strikingly similar decline in gross yield but a somewhat different behaviour of the net yield, which declined even more rapidly for the first kilometre but less precipitately thereafter. In like manner, Suomela (1950) discovered from an analysis of a sample of farms scattered all over Finland that the rapidity with which the net product declines diminishes as the distance increases.

Table 4 *Finland: relation of production per hectare and distance to farm plots (0–0.1 km equals 100)*

	Wiiala		Virri		Suomela
Distance (km)	gross output	net output	gross output	net output	net output
0–0.1	100	100	100	100	100
0.5	92	78	89	67	83
1.0	84	56	80	50	68
1.5	77	34	73	40	56
2.0	69	13	67	33	46
3.0	—	—	57	25	32
4.0	—	—	50	20	—
5.0	—	—	44	17	—

Sources: see text

That both the gross and net product should decline with diminishing rapidity at the greater distances is to be expected. The land near the farmstead receives considerable inputs of manure as well as of labour for cultivation and therefore a large proportion of the gross yield is attributable to factors other than the inherent fertility of the soil. With increasing distance, the various inputs of fertilizers and labour become smaller and therefore an increasing proportion of the total yield arises from the natural capacity of the land, until the point is reached that even with a minimal amount of care some level of production would be maintained. The data collected by Wiiala probably do not show this tendency owing to the fact that the maximum average distance with which he was concerned was not very great, being about 2 kilometres. Some rather similar, and more accessible, data are contained in Mead (1953), showing production costs at 1.0, 2.0 and 3.0 kilometres compared with costs adjacent to the farmstead.

It may be objected that the reduced yield obtained on the more distant lands is a result of either or both of two factors which are correlated with distance. First, the more distant land may be poorer. In the case of the three main sets of data quoted above, this was not a consideration which attracted the attention of the authors as being important, and they attribute the whole diminution to distance. In any case, the method which, perforce, they had to adopt precludes this as a serious likelihood. The book-keeping data were available only for each farm as a whole and not for individual fields, so that Wiiala's method of measuring distance was adopted. While it may be the case that on an individual farm the poorer land is at a greater remove than the better, there is no evidence to suggest that in general farms with a greater average distance to the plots possess inferior soils.

The second possible cross-correlation is that those farms with a greater average distance to the parcels were also larger farms. This would affect the intensity of production, for in general the per hectare level of gross and net income falls as farms increase in size. There is some evidence to show that in the case of Finland the larger farms do have greater average distances to their plots than the smaller but this is compensated in part by the fact that the plots are considerably larger, which has the effect of reducing the disadvantageous effects of distance. It appears, then, in the cases so far cited, that the major part of the fall in yield associated with distance is attributable to distance alone.

Using essentially the same technique with the accounts of 227 farms scattered over central Sweden, Larsson (1947) obtained very similar rates of decline for gross and net product. Examining the constitution of the farms, he concluded that the findings must be attributed primarily to the influence of distance and not to the quality of the soil or other factors. Table 5 is derived from his findings, which relate to the period 1939–43. Observe that the larger farms show a much more rapid decline for gross production than do the smaller holdings and that the converse situation holds for net product. The man with a small business must extract every bit of income he can from his property and therefore tends to push production to the maximum level possible on all his land. To maintain his level of gross output he must incur increasingly great costs of input as the distance increases. The man with a larger enterprise does not have to worry so much about obtaining the maximum total income and can afford to adjust his farming more carefully, reducing very sharply his inputs on the more distant fields. His gross product falls, but not as rapidly as his inputs. Larsson commented that this is apparent in terms of land use, the larger farms tending to have more grazing land of an unintensive nature than do the smaller holdings.

Table 5 *Sweden: percentage reduction in output per hectare for each kilometre increase in distance from the farmstead*

Size group of farms (*hectares*)	Number of farms	Percentage decrease in output for 1 kilometre increase in distance	
		gross production	*net production*
10–20	95	4	74
20–40	85	9	50
over 40	47	26	46
average	—	13	57

Source: Larsson 1947

The evidence from Scandinavia is confirmed by Dutch studies of both fragmented farms (Visser 1950) and linear holdings (Takes 1958). The former indicated a diminution in gross output of 9 per cent for each kilometre, while the latter referred to 1.2–1.5 kilometres as the threshold beyond which inferior cultivation becomes apparent.

Most of the European evidence was obtained before full mechanization had been achieved; with motorized operations, the distance effect is probably much less acutely felt over the range of distances considered. However, as the following paragraphs will show, the orders of magnitude of the distance effect are highly relevant in other situations, where development lags behind Europe. A survey of fragmented smallholdings in the Punjab of Pakistan resulted in the following observation:

it was noticed that cultivation operations were adversely affected due to the existence of tiny plots situated at considerable distances. .... A previous investigation into this aspect estimated that the expenses of cultivation increase 'by 5.3 per cent for every 500 metres of distance for ploughing, from 20 to 25 per cent for the transport of manure and from 15 to 32 per cent for the transport of crops'. [Khan 1955, 8]

The only major operation omitted is that of tending the growing crops. It is evident that, if the intensity of farming remains constant at all distances, the total cost of cultivating land rises by over 20 per cent for every kilometre, which would have the effect of reducing the net product per hectare in like measure.

Finally, Richardson's (1974) careful study of rice cultivation on the coastal fringe of Guyana yielded data summarized in Table 6. At the time the fieldwork was undertaken, rice was cultivated both by hand and by mechanical means. In general, the hand methods prevailed near the farmstead, while mechanization characterized the more distant plots. The situation was further complicated by the fact that in two of the villages surveyed it was common to take two crops annually, mostly on the land nearest the dwellings, whereas one crop prevailed elsewhere. The data in Table 6 refer to annual labour input and yields. Given the mixture of technologies employed,

Table 6 *Padi rice cultivation in Guyana (0–0.1 km equals 100)*

Distance from dwelling to plot (km)	Labour input excluding travel time	Gross yield of rice
0.0–0.1	100	100
0.5	96	88
1.0	18	75
1.5	12	66
2.0	11	56
3.0	10	50
4.0	9.5	47
5.0	9	44

Source: Richardson 1974

it is not surprising that annual labour inputs drop very sharply indeed; the remarkable thing is the fact that gross output declines with distance at nearly the same rate as is evident in Table 4.

Although he did not specifically analyse yields per hectare (gross and net), Blaikie (1971) meticulously estimated the total labour requirements of various crops for four Indian villages, from which he could estimate the expected spatial distribution of crops for comparison with the actual pattern. For the two villages dependent upon rainfall for this cropping (i.e. very little or no irrigation), total labour input fell quite regularly to the maximum distance of approximately 6 kilometres. For comparison with Tables 3 and 6, the standardized labour input at 5.0 kilometres was only a little over 25 per cent of the level at 0–0.1 kilometre. His standardized labour inputs were obtained by calculating the total actual labour input for each crop (travel included) at each location and converting to a base of the average for that crop, in units of standard deviations about the mean. The spatial pattern of standardized labour inputs (component scores) for the village of Daiikera, within 80 kilometres of Delhi, is shown in Figure 3. This figure also shows the pattern of land use which results from the spatial variation in cultivation costs, and so provides a convenient link to the next stage of analysis.

To conclude this section, there is a considerable body of quantitative evidence to demonstrate the rate at which the level of gross and net product does in fact decline with increasing distance, evidence which gives a firm basis to the numerous qualitative references to the matter which may be found in the literature. The material which has been quoted applies to technical conditions which for the most part require pedestrian human location and the common use of draught animals for ploughing and the transport of goods, for the level of mechanization was not high at the time the studies were made. These conditions still obtain in much of Europe and even more widely in large tracts of the world; therefore, the above-quoted estimates of the economic effects of distance are of the utmost relevance.

Patterns of land use

So far, we have identified a clearly recognizable reduction in labour input with distance from the farmstead, associated with reduced gross and net yields. This general relationship is manifested spatially

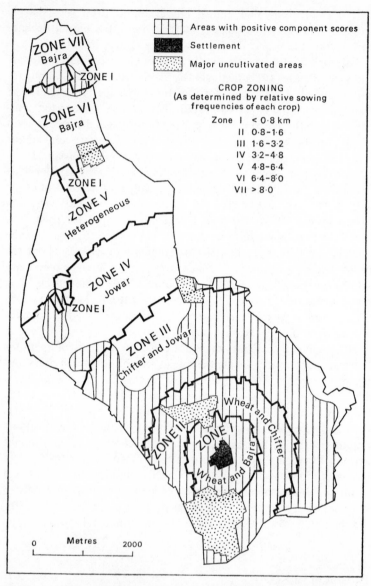

Figure 3   *India: crop zoning, village of Daiikera. Areas with positive component scores have above-average labour input.* Source: Blaikie 1971

in patterns of land use on the farm. Associated with lower labour inputs at greater distances is a reduction in the amount of fertilizer applied to the land (Draisma 1958; Blaikie 1971). This is a sufficient reason, though in fact by no means the only one, either for crop yields to decline with distance or for the pattern of cropping to vary spatially, so that the less labour-intensive uses of the land will be at the greater distances; or both adjustments may occur simultaneously.

Direct evidence on the relationship of yields per hectare to distance is extremely sparse in the published literature. On the other hand, there is a wealth of evidence to show that regularities are readily recognizable in the spatial arrangement of crops, cropping systems and livestock husbandry. The context in which these patterns can be identified the most easily is not the individual farm but a village territory, in which the settlement is nucleated and the farm holdings are fragmented and scattered over the territory; or land near the village is owned by the peasants (minifundia) while the more distant lands are held by large land-owners (latifundia); or thirdly, in some societies it is customary to work the land in common, in which case the whole village territory may be regarded for our present purpose as one big farm which has its own problems of spatial distribution. Whichever the case may be, the village or hamlet is the point from which emanate all the inputs which are applied to the land – notably labour – and the point to which all produce must be taken.

Figure 3 summarizes Blaikie's findings for one of his two Rajasthan villages, dependent upon dry farming. This study is probably the most careful published attempt to examine the validity of von Thünen's ideas at the village scale. From data on individual operations for specific crops, he estimated that the *extra* costs of cultivating land 914 metres from the dwelling, measured in man-days per hectare, rose as follows: wheat, 70 man-days; chifter, 40; jowar, 31; and bajra, 27. On the basis of this and kindred evidence, he established an 'expected' pattern of land use. Formal statistical tests showed that the actual land-use pattern, shown in Figure 3, correlated very closely indeed. Blaikie (1971, 16) concluded that 'the zoning reflects a movement-minimization strategy on the part of the cultivators'.

Numerous accounts have remarked upon the zoning of land uses around villages in Europe. South Italy and the islands of Sicily and Sardinia are characterized by a highly nucleated settlement pattern. The position as it was in the 1930s is shown in Table 7 but there has in fact been very little change to the present day, despite the post-war programme of land reform (see page 114). Thus, it is common for the peasantry to inhabit villages or agro-towns that reach a size of 10,000 persons and to have to travel daily to work the fields which surround the settlement. It is not our purpose to enquire how this pattern has arisen but to accept that, for such reasons as defence, avoidance of malaria and the system of land holding, it has come to pass. The consequences have been vividly described.

Table 7 *Italy, 1936: concentration of the rural population*

Region	Land area per inhabited centre (sq km)	Average distance between centres (km)	Average number of inhabitants per centre	Scattered population as percentage of that in centres
Apulia	53	7.3	6700	7.2
Sicily	33	5.7	4600	11.1
Basilicata	55	7.5	2600	15.1
Lazio	20	4.4	2400	25.0
Campania	11	3.3	2400	20.6
Sardinia	50	7.1	2000	8.7

Source: SVIMEZ 1950

large [Sicilian] settlements, where live practically all the peasants, are generally situated on hilltops or hill slopes, sometimes dominated by a ruined castle. . . .

Around these settlements there is a zone of intensive tree and herbaceous crop cultivation, in small fruit and vegetable plots, forming a 'halo' of greater or lesser extent according to the size of the village. Beyond this zone extend the former fiefs or latifundia, generally devoted to cereals and pasture.

The zone of intensive cultivation is composed of small or minute properties which are fragmented and dispersed and mostly derive from lease-hold concessions; they belong to all classes of the population – the wealthy, professional persons, wage workers, artisans and peasants. [Prestianni 1947, 98–9]

Despite the fact of being situated on hills, which means that the immediately adjacent land is generally of poor quality, the most intensive agriculture is conducted here. Rochefort (1961) noted that although manure was collected around the edges of the interior villages, it was applied to land only within a distance of one kilometre.

The same situation has been excellently noted in Sardinia, of the southern plains and plateaux:

From whichever side one leaves a village, one is struck by the rigorous disposition of the various elements of the countryside into concentric zones. Around the village ... there is a first zone in which the view is restricted, where the parcels are small and bounded by hedges of prickly pear, growing vegetables, olives, almonds and vines. But this pleasant labyrinth constitutes only a narrow belt, and suddenly there opens out a landscape which is flat and bare, without walls, without hedges, without trees: these are the arable lands. ... Completely cultivated in the area nearest the village, this territory becomes poorer in the distance, the amount of fallow increases. ... [le Lannou 1941, 188]

The deterioration of the landscape with increasing distance is attributed to the factor of distance and not to poorer natural conditions. Notice that the proportion of fallow land rises as the village is left behind, and that therefore the intensity of grain cultivation is falling.

Thanks to the publication by the Italian Touring Club of land-use maps of Italy, a more precise measurement is now possible than the above description of the arrangement of land uses around the rural centres. Canicatti is a settlement of 30,000 inhabitants, distant 18 kilometres from the nearest settlement of comparable size, typical of the larger centres in the interior of Sicily; for this reason it has been chosen for particular study. Table 8 has been compiled from the relevant sheet of the land-use map (scale 1:200,000), and from information supplied by the Istituto Nazionale di Economia Agraria in Rome regarding the annual labour requirements per hectare of particular crops. The distance zones have been taken from the centre of the settlement. The average labour requirement in each distance zone has been obtained from the data for the crops and the relative importance of each in the various zones.

The location of the small amount of irrigated and citrus lands is determined by the very limited area which is suitable. Apart from these two categories, the pattern of land use conforms to the descriptions which have been quoted, with a particularly marked diminution in the importance of vines, olives and arable-with-trees as the distance from the centre increases; the relative decline of the other tree crops is less marked. In this particular case, 4 kilometres is the critical

Table 8 Canicatti, Sicily: percentage of land area in various uses and annual labour requirements per hectare in man-days

Distance from Canicatti (km)	Percentage of land area										Average number of man-days per hectare in each distance zone
	urban	irrigated arable and vegetables	citrus fruits	vines	arable with trees	olive	trees*	arable, unirrigated	pasture and productive waste†	coppice wood	
0–1	44.7	—	—	15.8	—	—	19.7	19.7	—	—	52
1–2	—	—	—	18.0	16.7	8.4	41.0	15.9	—	—	50
2–3	—	—	2.6	2.3	21.8	14.4	35.4	23.6	—	—	46
3–4	—	—	2.1	13.3	18.7	0.6	47.2	18.1	—	—	50
4–5	—	—	—	5.1	19.2	2.4	28.4	43.4	1.4	—	42
5–6	—	1.0	—	6.3	4.7	1.6	17.6	64.1	4.7	—	41
6–7	1.3	0.7	—	3.3	6.7	—	18.3	68.7	0.9	—	40
7–8	—	—	—	4.0	7.7	—	23.6	62.4	0.8	1.6	39
Total	1.0	0.3	0.4	6.1	11.1	2.2	26.3	50.8	1.4	0.4	—
Average number of man-days per hectare		300	150	90	50	45	40	35	5	5	42

* Mainly almond, hazel, carob and pistacchio.
† Sometimes sown.

distance, beyond which open arable land (growing mostly wheat and barley) becomes predominant. Also evident is the decline in the amount of labour applied to each hectare as the distance increases, with again a sharp change at about 4 kilometres. The actual diminution of labour input is undoubtedly much greater than is indicated, for two closely related reasons. First, it has been assumed that the actual labour input remains the same for each crop irrespective of the distance from the centre, an assumption which is evidently not reliable, as we have previously seen. But the data with which to allow for this are not available. Second, the arable land tends to be left in fallow more frequently at greater distances and when so left requires very little attention. Thus the right-hand column of the table should be interpreted in the following manner: it indicates the minimum rate of reduction of labour inputs with increasing distance, and measures the magnitude of the labour economy which is actually achieved solely by the substitution of less demanding crops towards the periphery of the commune's territory, taking no account of variations in the intensity with which individual crops are grown.

Exactly the same type of situation has been noted in Spain. Of La Mancha, a particularly arid part of the Meseta south of Madrid, Birot and Dresch observed:

On a terrain which is almost perfectly homogeneous . . . the pattern of settlement and land use is remarkably geometric. In the middle of the nude plain there are enormous villages, at times numbering only 4 or 5 in 600 square kilometres. Around the villages, the bare fields on the one hand and the olives and vines on the other are disposed in concentric circles. The latter crops [olives and vines], covering an important area, generally are not found nearer the village than 3 or 4 kilometres. There is a third and outer ring, the uncleared land abutting on the surrounding hills. In sum, there has been an annual clearance about the initial centre, devoted to grain or tree crops according to the needs of the population and the state of the market. [Birot and Dresch 1953, 218]

That the figure of 3–4 kilometres should be mentioned as the critical distance separating the grain fields from the olives and vines, which is roughly the same figure obtained for Canicatti, is probably a coincidence. Much more interesting is the inversion of the spatial distribution, the arable land being close to the settlement. This may be attributed to two major considerations: in La Mancha there has not been the same fragmentation of the land into small holdings adjacent to the settlement as in Italy; and under the more severe climatic conditions the labour requirement per hectare for wheat and barley is higher than for vines and olives. The latter point was succinctly made in a study of one particular Spanish village:

This peripheral distribution [of vines and olives] is due to the fact that the cultivation of cereals requires more frequent application of labour than does the cultivation of vines and olives; this makes it more convenient for the labourer to live nearer the arable land than the vine and olive plots, in order to reduce the time lost in travelling from his home in the village to the land he works. [Pons 1956, 190–1]

Comparison of the Italian and Spanish material illustrates an important consideration of wide application: the relative labour requirements of the same crops are very variable from place to place and hence the relative spatial arrangement of land uses. This is clear from data supplied by the Istituto Nazionale di Economia Agraria, Rome, a selection of which is presented in Table 9, showing the annual labour requirements per hectare for certain crops as a percentage of the requirement for wheat and barley, in different parts of Italy. The broad pattern remains constant: irrigated vegetables always require a lot of labour and chestnuts very little; vines need more attention than olives. But the relative position of tobacco, tomatoes and vines is much more variable from place to place. That such large differences in the relative labour needs of crops occur within the

Table 9 *Italy: annual labour requirements in man-days per hectare* (*wheat and barley equals 100*)

Crop	Aosta	Pavia	Genoa	Arezzo	Latina	Bari	Syracuse
wheat and barley	100	100	100	100	100	100	100
irrigated vegetables	2390	1020	1440	500	960	1250	860
tobacco	—	155	—	—	340–510	710	—
tomatoes	—	195	450	—	240	—	240–760
vines	700	400	360	240	320–390	320–360	290
olives	—	—	125	160	70	180	140
chestnuts	60	—	45	35	33	—	—

Source: Istituto Nazionale di Economia Agraria, Rome

confines of a single country shows conclusively the necessity for analysing local conditions carefully and the danger of applying in one place preconceptions based on experience elsewhere.

It may be objected that the cases of zoning which have been cited so far are very special and localized. In the next few paragraphs it is shown that the same type of phenomenon is observed elsewhere. South Spain and south Italy (with Sicily and Sardinia) represent in an extreme form the concentration of the rural population into large agrotowns but the same situation prevails to a lesser degree over much of Europe. This has been clearly shown by Dovring (1965*a*), who has mapped the areas of various median village sizes in Europe and European Russia. Outside the two Mediterranean countries already mentioned, the median size of village is over 1000 inhabitants in extensive tracts of Yugoslavia, Bulgaria, Romania, the Ukraine and the area immediately north of the Caucasus: the latter region can boast a median size of over 5000, comparable with parts of Italy and Spain. Hungary also is a country of sizeable 'villages', with one-fifth of the *total* population living in settlements of between 3000 and 9999; between 1960 and 1970, settlements below 5000 were in general declining (Vörösmarti 1976).

Hence, it is no surprise to discover that in parts of Bulgaria the zoning of production around the villages has been observed as occurring generally. Birot and Dresch (1953) refer to the phenomenon, stating that the farms are only loosely grouped into villages and are each adjacent to a plot of land used for growing vegetables, fruits, some vines and cotton. Then, very close to the village, some communal pasture lands and woodlots are found and beyond them the specialized crops which require larger amounts of labour – vines, roses and tobacco. Next again come fields farmed on a two-year rotation, supporting arable crops like wheat and maize. At the edge of the territory there may be some pioneer vineyards or rose gardens nibbling away at the forest. This description relates to the situation which subsisted before the Communist government came to power, before the organization of the agricultural lands under the collective-farm system which is now virtually complete in Bulgaria. To the extent that this policy has had any effect on the settlement pattern, the tendency has been to encourage the maintenance of nucleation, even to exaggerate it further, as one means of controlling and influencing the rural populace.

Policy in the USSR has tended in the same direction, though the disadvantageous economic consequences have been realized and some move made to mitigate the extreme ill-effects. Thus, the observation of de Laveleye (1901, 12) that 'more cognizance is taken of proximity than of the [natural] fertility, since in Russia this does not vary much within each region' has been endorsed by subsequent writers and is still generally true, giving rise to a concentric arrangement of land uses.

Africa supplies us with the largest number of accounts of land-use zoning around settlements. One of the earliest appeared just after the Second World War, referring to the village of Agogo, situated east of Kumasi and possessing a population of 4500. Steel (1947, 159) noted

the clear distinction between the area within a mile or so of the town, where are most of the food-farms, and the zone beyond which is mainly under cocoa. This is partly to be explained by the ecological conditions, and partly by the fact that food-farms need to be visited at frequent intervals throughout the year while cocoa once established needs very little attention, no more than an occasional weeding between the trees and the plucking of the pods when ripe.

One of the more renowned accounts was published ten years later (Prothero 1957), describing the village of Soba in northern Nigeria. Four important categories of land use may be distinguished. Within the village walls, the dwellings are intermingled with 'gardens' where vegetables, culinary herbs and the like are grown in great profusion and apparent confusion, with close interplanting and careful catch-cropping. Such 'gardens' require frequent visits, if only to pluck produce for the next meal, and they receive manure to enable cultivation to proceed year in and year out. Outside the walls, continuously cropped land extends to a distance of 0.8–1.2 kilometres, fertilized with manure and the droppings of the migrant cattle which are kraaled there, growing the staple crops of Guinea corn, cotton, tobacco and groundnuts. Beyond that again is a zone varying in width from 0.8 to 1.6 kilometres which is under rotation farming, the land being cultivated for three to four years and then allowed to revert to bush for at least five years, to restore the fertility which would otherwise be entirely destroyed in the absence of manure. Fourth comes the heavy bush in which there are small clearings around isolated settlements, these clearings reproducing the sequence described above. From the account given by Prothero, it is evident that this general arrangement arises from the problems posed by distance, though the quality of the terrain modifies the theoretical symmetry.

That these two examples are representative of a phenomenon which occurs widely throughout the African continent is shown by the large number of cases described by Sautter (1962), the case studies edited by Ruthenberg (1968), essays by Morgan (1969 and 1973) and the special issue of *Études Rurales* in 1970. Numerous other studies have been published and it would be tedious to extend the catalogue. However, two points are worth making about some of the more recent studies. The first is to note the emergence of quantitative data. Lericollais (1970) collected data on the production of millet/sorghum and groundnuts in the village of Sob, Senegal. The output, in kilograms per hectare of *all* land, was at a maximum of 406 for millet/sorghum within a radius of 0.5 kilometre, falling more or less continuously to 71 kilograms at distances in excess of 3 kilometres. Although groundnuts were also grown near the village the maximum output of 297 kilograms per gross hectare was in the zone 0.5–1.0 kilometre, thereafter declining to 71 beyond 3 kilometres. This pattern reflected the availability of manure, the relative labour requirements of the crops and the frequency of fallow. Under rather similar environmental conditions in northern Nigeria, Norman (1973) obtained the land-use data shown in Table 10, indicating an adjustment of land use over distances substantially shorter than reported in other studies. In the even more arid area of south Chad studied by Gilg (1970), at distances between 3 and 4 kilometres three-quarters of the land used by the inhabitants of Dobadene was in bush

Table 10 *Land-use data for three Hausa villages, northern Nigeria, per cent of area*

| | Distance from compound, metres | | | |
	< 183	*183–269*	*> 269*	*total*
total cropped area	32.4	34.0	33.6	100.0
millet	52.5	21.5	27.0	100.0
fallow	17.1	36.9	46.0	100.0
cotton	9.5	14.5	76.0	100.0

Source: Norman 1973

savanna or cultivated with fallow periods in excess of two years, whereas shorter fallows were more common closer to the village. Finally a sample survey of households covering the entire eastern region of Ghana showed that for cocoa-growing households the *maximum* distance to the cocoa farms was less than 4 kilometres in 69 per cent of cases and exceeded 6 kilometres for only 10 households in every hundred (Bhattacharya and Potakey 1969).

The second point of interest follows from Morgan's (1969) observation that most of the cases of obvious land-use zoning around African villages occur in the savanna zone, and especially in West Africa. In the more humid rain-forest regions, maps of land use do not reveal the same pattern to anything like the same degree. Almost certainly the primary reason lies in the complexity of the relationships between settlements and land use and the need, in certain circumstances, to concentrate on individual holdings. Furthermore, it may be necessary to distinguish explicitly between crops grown by men and those tended by women. Tindituuza and Kateete (1971) report very serious fragmentation of land holdings despite a dispersed pattern of settlement. Within the Kigezi District, which lies in the extreme south-west of Uganda, coffee and tobacco are grown by the men as cash crops. On each holding, these crops are grown nearest the dwelling, while the women are obliged to use more distant plots for food crops. An equally interesting case has been reported by Jackson (1970) from the extreme south-western edge of the Ethiopian plateau. Considerable local relief creates a wide range of environmental conditions, allowing a mixture of arable and livestock farming. Farms are fragmented, the most distant plots being between 1 and $1\frac{1}{2}$ hours' travel time from the dwellings. The poorer peasants have so little land that each plot must be devoted to that crop for which it is most suited, irrespective of its distance. The few head of cattle are stabled near the dwelling. As some crops must be manured, manure is in fact carried to some of the most distant plots, past land which receives no manure. By contrast, the richer peasants have sufficient cattle to warrant satellite dwellings and are able to minimize their work effort of applying the manure on land near these byres. For these richer peasants, a complex pattern of land use results which serves to minimize labour inputs. However, as the richer and poorer peasants work side by side, simple land-use mapping will not reveal the reality; it is necessary to treat the individual holdings as functional units.

By now, enough evidence has been cited in detail to show that the zoning of land use around settlements is a widespread phenomenon. Other authors have identified similar phenomena in Uttar Pradesh (Ahmad 1952) and Sri Lanka (Öhrling 1977). But perhaps the last word may be left with a former member of the Indian Civil Service, who as long ago as 1912, had recognized the generality of the zoning in the then United Provinces:

The fields nearest the site are most often manured: fields lying a little further off are manured occasionally, and those at the greatest distance get no manure at all. The result is obvious to the eye when the crops are on the ground: each group of houses is a centre from which the fertility gradually decreases to the outskirts of the land depending on the village or hamlet. The most remunerative crops are found near the houses and the inferior crops further off. [Moreland 1912, 45]

Arising from the above analysis, some further points deserve attention. Doubtless it has already occurred to the reader that some of the cases which have been cited are examples of the infield–outfield system that was common in much of western Europe throughout the Middle Ages and later (Slicher van Bath 1963; Smith 1967). This point was explicitly made by Allan (1965) in the context of northern Ghana but has a general application. As the very name indicates, this was an agricultural system built upon two foundations: the infield was that land near the dwellings which was in continuous cultivation year after year; the outfield was the territory which lay further off and though subject to the plough was given periodic respite. Though much the same crops might be grown on both the infield and the outfield, the former received manure, whereas the latter had to rely upon periods of fallow to restore its fertility. Essentially, this was a system providing two levels of intensity of arable use, with a third zone of more extensive exploitation as grazing lying beyond. In Yorkshire, the nearer 'part of the township commanded a higher rent than land in the outfield and was also preferred to other parts of the open fields when new crops came to be introduced' (Harris 1961, 25). Some infield–outfield farming has survived to modern times in Ireland, allowing contemporary observation to confirm the historical documentation and inference (McCourt 1958).

So far, the discussion has been conducted with the implicit assumption that settlements are permanent and immovable. For something approaching 200 million people, scattered mainly throughout Africa, parts of South America and Australasia, shifting cultivation is the norm and is associated with frequent relocation of dwellings (Grigg 1974). One of the classic studies of shifting cultivation is that by de Schlippé (1956), who described the Zande system before forcible permanency of settlement was imposed (Reinig 1970; Sautter 1975). In selecting a new site, the Azande invariably choose to build their home on the most fertile type of soil which forms one band in the catena that rises from the valley floor to the crest of the interfluve. Once the settlement is established, two types of land use quickly develop. The first is immediately adjacent to the homestead and consists of the permanent cultivation of a mélange of crops, with the application of manures and garbage to maintain fertility. Beyond this zone, which is confined to the fertile band of the soil catena, a more extensive system prevails – in all directions, and, therefore, on the more fertile soil as well as the less bountiful. The bush is cleared annually, cassava, millet and other crops are planted, and the land may then be allowed to revert to bush or it may be cleared for another crop. From the maps de Schlippé compiled showing the areas actually cultivated each year, it is readily apparent that the following pattern exists. Immediately beyond the zone which is continuously cultivated, the land is in fact put under crops practically every year. As the distance from the homestead increases, the frequency with which the same plot is cleared diminishes, until it may be sown only once. Although there is no change in the type of crop being grown, the intensity of land use steadily diminishes in all directions.

As time passes, the unfertilized lands which are nearest the homestead become exhausted and cultivation must be pushed ever further afield, with the consequence that the cost of cultivation – as measured by the amount of labour required to produce a given quantity of goods – rises. The point comes when it is worth while to remove the whole household to a new site, since the cost of resettling will be fully compensated by the saving in cultivation costs. That this is indeed the case is confirmed by Brookfield's (1973) finding that the Chimbu of New Guinea re-locate their dwelling when the distance separating it from the central point in the garden plots exceeds 1.4 kilometres.

Shifting cultivation is one response to the problem of soil degradation around settlements, a problem which has already been referred to in the context of permanent settlements, where serious soil erosion may be the long-term outcome (page 32). Indeed, Ancey (1974) found that a sample of villages in the Ivory Coast, examined over the period 1900 to 1970, were being re-located once every century on average, probably as a response to the exhaustion of the soil. Shifting cultivators respond to this problem by abandoning the land for a period of regeneration, prior to clearance and further use, over a relatively short cycle.

Some of the worse effects of extreme fragmentation may be avoided in the following manner. One peasant may let some of his further plots to another, from whose farmstead the plots are more accessible. The first peasant may then rent some land on the same basis, either from his partner in the first transaction or from a third party. In this way, although the pattern of *ownership* means that some parcels are far removed from the farmsteads, the pattern of *operation* is not so unfavourable. Contemporary examples of this happening have been reported from Almeria in Spain (Llobet 1958), from Kenya (Republic of Kenya 1966), India (Agarwal 1971), Sri Lanka (Ganewatte 1974) and Taiwan (Meer 1975). Precisely the same thing occurred under the open-field system of pre-Parliamentary enclosure English farming, apparently as a step towards the consolidation of holdings (van Bath 1963). Meer's study in Taiwan suggests that complex interlocking ownership rights are also a step in the same direction. (See also page 116.) Yet another response to the problems posed by fragmentation and ownership rights has been reported from Jamaica. If it is necessary to grow bulky crops on distant plots, these will be sold in the field to dealers known as 'higglers' thus avoiding the cost of transporting the produce to the farmstead (Edwards 1961).

Under-employment and unemployment

The basis of the argument in this chapter has been the proposition that human labour is scarce, and that human energies may be bent upon several competing ends. From this position it has been argued that an attempt will be made to equate the cost of the last dose of labour with the benefits which accrue from it. Now it is commonly held that this fundamental assumption ceases to be valid in circumstances where labour is unemployed or under-employed; human time saved in one process of cultivation adds nothing to the general welfare, there being no productive use to which it can be put. If this were so, no kind of zoning would be apparent, because all the territory would be farmed to the same level of intensity.

An individual peasant operating his own land may have one member of his family unemployed. It will then be worth while to raise the general level of intensity of land use much above the level which would otherwise prevail, since every small addition to the total product is clear gain in economic terms. However, poverty is relative to what one is accustomed to receive and one's ideas about what is right, and the point will be reached when it is preferable to sit in the shade and have social intercourse than to toil in the sun for a pittance. Very rarely indeed will the marginal product of labour be zero; for it to approach that value, poverty must be desperate indeed (Brown and Salkin 1974). But more important, whatever the general level of intensity achieved, it will still remain advantageous to obtain an equal marginal return from the marginal input on each plot, since otherwise production could be raised with no increase in labour, merely by a spatial readjustment of the level of inputs. Thus it will still be desirable to arrange the spatial pattern of production in accordance with the principles we have been propounding, though the general level of intensity will be higher than under conditions of full employment, where there are alternative occupations.

Where there is unemployment, the same will be true of hired labour, which may receive only a pittance for a day's work. For the person who hires the workers it is clearly desirable that the amount of time actually spent at work and not travelling should be as great as possible, which puts a premium upon the more intensive use of the nearer land.

Where the unemployment is seasonal and not continued throughout the year, the argument presented in this chapter also remains intact. The farming system will be geared to the availability of labour at the times of peak demand – usually at seeding and harvest times – when there is generally an actual shortage of manpower (Clark and Haswell 1970). The disposition of land uses will be adjusted to this situation of seasonally scarce labour.

In this context, note that in southern Italy, Sicily, Sardinia and Spain there is a great deal of rural unemployment – indeed, in this respect these areas are notorious. However, the spatial zoning of cultivation is here more strikingly apparent than in most of the rest of Europe. Similarly, seasonal unemployment and under-employment is characteristic of Africa, the Indian sub-continent and elsewhere. We may conclude, therefore, that in fact the relative spatial disposition of land uses will not be affected by the existence of un-employment or under-employment.

Conclusion

To end this chapter, it will be useful to summarize very briefly the conclusions which emerge. It is quite apparent that the problem of distance is sufficiently great for there to be a response in the patterns of land use on farms and around villages in all parts of the world, as a common phenomenon. We have also been able to gain some idea of the magnitude of the effect upon gross and net production. The Finnish data, for example, showed a very rapid diminution with distance, while the Dutch and Pakistani material displayed a some-what less precipitate decline. In view of the difficulty of working with the kind of material which is available, this difference need cause no surprise. All these studies agree in showing that at a distance of 1 kilometre the decline in net return is large enough to be significant as a factor adversely affecting the prosperity of the farming popu-lation, and this order of magnitude corresponds with the opinions quoted by Dovring. These quantitative data on money returns indi-cate that, at about 3–4 kilometres, the costs of operation rise suffi-ciently to be oppressive and seriously detrimental, and in general the descriptive material quoted tends to confirm that it is exceptional for distances greatly to exceed this limit with any frequency.

Some qualification to the above conclusion is necessary. If we consider the *limiting distance*, beyond which agriculturalists are un-willing to travel on a daily or semi-daily basis, there does appear to be some relationship with the size of settlement nucleations and the pressure of population. Where, as in parts of Europe and Africa, nucleations in excess of 5000 inhabitants are common and pressure on resources is severe, the limiting distance is frequently of the order 6–11 kilometres (Morgan 1969). Under semi-arid conditions in India, Blaikie (1971) found that 10 kilometres was the limiting dis-tance, whereas under more humid conditions and more intensive farming, 3–5.5 kilometres represents the maximum radius. By con-trast, Melanesian peoples generally regard 4.5 kilometres or there-abouts as the greatest distance that is acceptable, in some cases less (Brookfield and Hart 1971). Certainly, the present author was impressed by the unwillingness of the inhabitants of New Guinea to undertake labours that would seem commonplace elsewhere in the world; but there was no necessity, owing to low pressure of population on resources.

4 The region and the world: 1

At the small scale of phenomenon – the farm and village – it was noted that the cost of overcoming distance arises largely, if not exclusively, from the amount of human time expended, both in accompanying all inputs and produce and in transferring from one site of operations to another. Therefore, it is possible to measure costs directly in terms of man-hours, or if preferred these may be converted into monetary costs. With the larger scales of location, the costs caused by distance are expressed directly in cash terms and, in the present context, pertain much more to the movement of goods than to persons. Transport services may be obtained from private or public companies for a cash payment, or they may be provided by the firm itself. In the latter case a monetary outlay is necessary to purchase, maintain and run the vehicles, and so transport costs are measured directly in cash terms.

Though cost is the main consideration, time does still have considerable importance. Many agricultural products are highly perishable: either they must be marketed within relatively few hours of being uprooted, or preservative devices must be applied to prolong the life of the fruits, meat or dairy produce. The most important of these devices is refrigeration, for which new applications continue to be found; but note also the growing use of inert gases, as in the preservation of dessert apples. However, these techniques add to the cost of transport by simultaneously raising the capital outlay on rolling stock (or ships) and terminal facilities and reducing the useful load which may be carried. In the absence of such precautions, the costs imposed by time are measurable in terms of the deterioration of the produce, with high wastage and reduced unit value.

Time also has an effect on insurance costs, since insurance rates in transit are greater than in store, so that the longer a commodity is in movement the greater the costs incurred on that account. The more rapidly a vehicle travels, the greater is its productivity in terms of tonne-kilometres or passenger-kilometres, and this is one factor affecting the level of charges. These considerations and others relating to time are reflected in the level of charges levied upon goods and passengers and need not be considered separately.

It is of fundamental importance to distinguish between the charge which is levied for a transport service and the costs which are involved in providing that service. There is no necessary relationship, as is apparent from any of the standard textbooks on the economics of transport. That which is charged by the transport company is a cost to the firm consigning the goods and in the discussion which follows the term 'cost' will be used in this sense. After all, our decisions about the use of transport facilities are based on what it costs us, and not upon an estimate of the expenses incurred by the transport company. This is illustrated by the reduction of railway rates on grain consigned from Chicago and elsewhere to ports on the eastern littoral of the United States in 1959 with the opening of the St Lawrence Seaway, a competing medium of transport offering lower rates than formerly obtained on the railways.

Although it is now widely accepted that transport costs are not a major factor in the location of many manufacturing industries in countries such as the United Kingdom (Brown 1969; Chisholm 1971; Edwards 1969 and 1970), this conclusion does not apply to the agricultural sector, especially when a continental or world view is adopted. The United States Department of Agriculture (1969) found that in 1959 the cost of rail transport averaged 8.2 per cent of the wholesale value at destination of agricultural products, and 4.0 per cent for animals and livestock. Of the twelve semi-perishable products identified, the lowest incidence was 2.2 per cent and the highest 17.1 per cent (cotton in bales, and barley and rye, respectively). Among the perishable products, the comparable figures were 2.0 for fresh berries and 37.5 for water-melons. The data series were discontinued in 1959. However, within the European Economic Community, French producers of wine, fruit and vegetables have been seriously perturbed by the competitive advantage in northerly markets (mainly Germany) enjoyed by Italian rivals, an advantage conferred by illogicalities in the railway tariff structure, such that international rail charges from Italy are substantially lower than from French shipping points (Bourrinet 1971).

A second difference distinguishing the smaller and larger scales of phenomena is that the point to which produce is taken ceases generally to be the same spot from which the inputs emanate. For example, the sugar beet of East Anglian farmers is sent to the factories of the British Sugar Corporation, but fertilizers, animal feeds and machinery are bought from dealers in other locations. Or New Zealand buys most of her agricultural machinery imports from the United Kingdom and western Europe while selling an increasing proportion of her farm products to the Asiatic countries. Hence, the response to distance arising from the marketing of produce will give rise to a pattern related to one set of points, while the pattern related to inputs is based upon another set of points. The resultant organization is therefore vastly more complex than in the smaller scales already discussed, though in principle this same problem obtrudes there too, but, as we have seen, it is of minor importance.

A further consideration is the sheer size of many conurbations, whether London or Tokyo. These extensive urban areas constitute the main destinations of much agricultural produce and the source of many farming requisites, such as machinery. Clearly, we cannot assume these conurbations to be mere points without some justification. They can only be treated as points for the purposes of our study if a sufficiently sizeable section of the world, or the whole globe, is taken into account. Even the largest conurbations then dwindle into insignificant little blobs. A case will make this clearer. Viewed from London, the coast of Europe is dotted with many ports, to each of which a distinct freight rate prevails on any particular commodity. Each port – whether Rotterdam or Hamburg – has its own unique space-relationships within the European scene. Looked at from New Zealand or Australia by an exporter of butter or meat, these differences become of negligible importance; in fact, it is normal for the shipping companies to quote rates which are identical for all the ports of north-west Europe. For practical purposes, therefore, this part of the world coalesces to form a single minute area which may justifiably be regarded as a point when considering certain aspects of international trade and world production patterns.

When dealing with large regions, or the whole world, a vast range of geological, topographical, climatic and political conditions is brought within our purview. For this reason, it is foolish to expect the single factor of distance – which is not even geographical distance but is economic distance, related to transport charges – to account for all phenomena, or even always to provide readily discernible regularities. The purpose of the rest of this chapter is to show how, within the milieu of physical environment and political circumstances, the problem of overcoming distance does confer a good deal of logic to spatial distributions. A beginning will be made with a simple situation, the existence of a single line of communication through a territory and the patterns of land use which develop as a consequence; thereafter, attention will be directed towards the large urban agglomerations, taking the case of the United Kingdom as an example, followed by reference to other examples elsewhere in the world.

A single transport route

A railway line is accessible only at selected points, the stations, whereas the majority of roads open up continuous access on both sides. Rivers and canals are also variously accessible, either at a few points or very many. Nevertheless, at the regional scale of analysis, we may treat all overland modes of transport, except air, as providing access along a continuous line. Where the communication network is sparse, zones of land use may be expected, parallel to the transport routes and dependent upon access thereto. The following paragraphs describe some important examples of such land-use zoning, and indicate briefly how information of this kind can be used for the evaluation of transport investments.

An interesting case is found in English history, relating to the supply of timber and having important repercussions on the course of economic and military affairs. Before the advent of iron, steel and concrete, timber was a universally important construction material, alike for ships and houses; before coal and coke came into general use, wood and charcoal were the chief fuels. During the sixteenth and seventeenth centuries, the rate of consumption outstripped the supply available from home resources and shortages of all types of timber became acute. Writing of ship timber, Albion (1926, 102) observed that:

when the period of shortage came, there was still plenty of good oak in England, but much of it was inaccessible. Twenty miles [32 kilometres] was ordinarily considered a maximum [overland] haul. Beyond that distance land carriage added heavily to the cost of timber, so that in the more remote localities many great oaks which would have made splendid ship timber were cut up for ordinary carpenter's purposes. The strips of woodland within fifteen or twenty miles [24–32 kilometres] of the coast or navigable rivers were the first places to be exploited for timber.

The significance of this problem of overland transport for timber can easily be appreciated from the maps which Willan (1936) has prepared, showing those areas of England and Wales situated more than 24 kilometres from navigable waters at various dates. Considerable tracts of southern England, where grew the finest ship timber, and much of the central and northern portions of the country were at a greater remove from passable waters and therefore were under-exploited or neglected entirely, except to supply local needs. Confirmation of the point is found in an Act early in the reign of Elizabeth I forbidding iron workers to use trees of more than 0.3 of a metre in diameter within 22 kilometres of the sea; but this was not successful in its object, namely the preservation of timber supplies for ship construction.

A more recent, and excellently documented case, is the settlement of the prairies of North America in the railway era. Apart from railways, overland transport was conducted by horse and cart, which severely restricted the distance over which it was economic to transport wheat from the farm to the station. Mackintosh (1934) devoted a chapter to the relationship between the pattern of settlement and the construction of railways in the Canadian prairies, from which certain main conclusions emerge. New settlement for agricultural purposes was mostly confined to land within reach of an existing railway, or near the alignment of a projected or anticipated route. A fair proportion of this settlement may have been by 'profit-takers', who sold the holding when the capital asset could be realized, after the railway had been built, moving on to anticipate further construction (Fishlow 1965). Thus, while it was common for settlers to cart their wheat as much as 80 kilometres, this was only done in the expectation that subsequent railway construction would reduce the haul to railhead to between 16 and 24 kilometres at the most. Greater distances were found not to be economic on a long-term basis and consequently the railway companies found it advantageous to construct a network sufficiently dense for most land to be contained within belts extending to 16 kilometres on either hand. Where the distance remained permanently greater than this, the cost of wagon carriage of wheat rendered it unprofitable to market and it was common for farmers so situated to convert the grain into livestock, which, being able to walk, could better support the cost of transport to railhead.

The same phenomenon has been described in Australia, where in the wheat belt railways now generally serve a territory extending about 24 kilometres on either side. During the 1890s, the economic limit of haul to the nearest station varied according to the price received by the farmers for their wheat: at a price of 3s. or 2s. 9d. a bushel, it was scarcely worth growing grain even under 16 kilometres from the railway, but with a price of 4s. 8d. the tributary zone extended to nearly 50 kilometres (Dunsdorfs 1956). Grazing occupied the more distant lands.

Much of Africa, south and central America, large areas of Asia, Borneo, New Guinea and elsewhere have never witnessed modern forms of transport, or possess but rudimentary networks. Here are ideal conditions in which zoning about single lines of communication can and does occur. It will be many decades before such economies become sufficiently complex and developed for the simple zoning to disappear. Of the numerous examples it will suffice to quote only a few, ample to establish the point.

A very well documented case is that of the railway which runs from Port Franqui on the river Kasai, a tributary of the Congo, to the Katanga Province of the former Belgian Congo. Nicolaï and Jacques (1954), in their study of this 1100-kilometre route, noted that whereas in the 1920s, when the route was built, many of the regions through which it passes were empty of people or but sparsely inhabited, in 1951 some 23 per cent of the population in the administrative areas traversed lived in but 5 per cent of the land area in a belt extending only 2.5 kilometres on either side of the railway. Examining the reasons for this change in the distribution of population, they conclude that it is largely due to immigration into the zone adjacent to the railway:

It is undeniable that the narrow strip which borders the railway has experienced growth of population, by the establishment of numerous villages peopled by immigrants . . . and by the development of a series of urban centres . . . where absolutely no important towns existed before 1922. [Nicolaï and Jacques 1954, 47]

Many of the immigrants were labourers who worked on the railway and then chose to settle locally instead of returning home. An important attraction was the possibility of engaging in commercial agriculture for sale. The result has been the development of alimentary crops – notably cassava – for sale in the mining areas of Katanga and of crops such as cotton and more recently rubber and coffee for export abroad. The prices of these products decline with distance from the railway, as is illustrated by the case of cassava in the Kasai region:

Distance from railway (km)	Price (francs per kg)
up to 15	1.5
15–30	1.45
90–105	1.2
105–120	1.15
135–150	1.05
over 150	1.00

The foodcrops are relatively bulky and of low unit value and so derive the greatest advantage from being near the transport artery. Hence, there is an inner zone of these crops – where, incidentally, farms are very small – and the cotton cultivation is found further away. As a result of the growth of population and the expansion of cash sales in conjunction with static agricultural techniques, severe degradation of the soil is taking place in the most favourably located areas which are the most intensively used, while the remoter parts remain in forest.

Numerous other studies attest to the spatial impact of single lines of communication. Bonney (1964) found that in Sabah, Borneo, development extended only 8 km either side of roads, whereas Borchert's (1967) study of Angola, conducted prior to the civil war of the 1970s, showed that profitable development could rarely occur more than 50 km from the railways which penetrated inland. The growth of Ecuador's banana industry, from relative unimportance to become the world's leading exporter, depended on the provision of road access. 'Wherever conditions permit, banana farms line these new travel arteries' (Parsons 1957, 204; see also Preston 1965). Beyond this strip of farmed territory lies the undisturbed forest, where transport costs are too high to permit cultivation. A 1962 account of agriculture in Ghana noted how the construction of modern transport facilities has resulted in the land-use pattern taking on a 'ribbon-like appearance, the zones of cultivation [being] aligned along the roads' (Wills 1962, 177). Perhaps the most vivid example is provided by Soja's (1968) generalization of the spatial pattern of economic and political development in Kenya in the early 1960s, as portrayed in Figure 4.

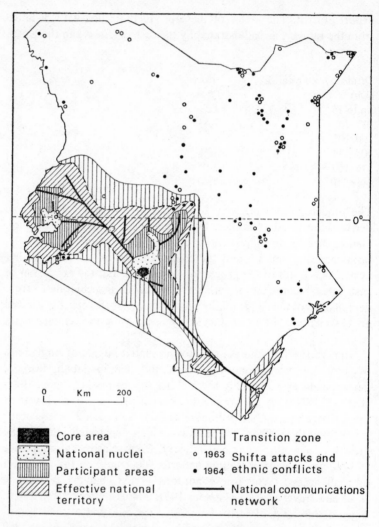

Figure 4 *Kenya: spatial pattern of development in the early 1960s.* **Source:** Soja 1968

The most dramatic contemporary example of the opening up of virgin lands is in the Amazon Basin, by the construction of a road network in the Brazilian portion and by the pushing of communications eastwards from the Andean states. In the ten years to 1977, the Brazilians built over 11,000 km of roads, whereby a cattle herd of six million head has been built up; one million new settlers have moved in (*The Times*, 13 December 1977). Although there must be grave doubts about the ecological damage being done and the long-term viability of much of the agricultural development (Manshard 1975; Goodland and Irwin 1975), the geographical impact has been impressive. The main road runs westwards from the existing route from Recife to Pôrto Franco on the eastern edge of the Basin, skirting southwards of the Amazon River itself to reach almost to the border of Peru at Cruzeiro do Sul. By Presidential decree, a strip of land 100 km wide on either side of the main roads has been reserved for agriculture. In practice, the *planned* colonization of agriculturalists is taking place in settlements within about 20 km of main roads, while *unplanned* slash-and-burn subsistence farmers have moved into the less accessible regions.

Meantime, less dramatic but nevertheless important inroads have been made into the Amazonian forests from the Andean states (Nelson 1973; Crist and Nissly 1973; Preston 1974). The greater part of this colonization is spontaneous, as farmers quit the overcrowded highlands in search of cultivable territory. Consequently, quantitative data are sparse. As roads are built into the lowlands, settlers take up land along the highways and the navigable rivers that are brought into communication with the populous mountain zone. The overall scale of this process is indicated by the fact that around Caranavi, 100 km north-east of La Paz, the population within 30 km of the road grew from virtually zero in 1945 to 36,000 in 1967 (Nelson 1973). It seems likely that taking the two countries mainly involved (Bolivia and Colombia), the total number of settlers must run to several hundred thousand; at least some part of this colonization occurs in anticipation of road construction, as previously noted in the North American prairies (page 67).

Let us return for a moment to the former Belgian Congo. Nicolaï and Jacques noted that a marked concentration of population had occurred in a strip of territory along the railway. As in the case of other studies cited above, much of this population augmentation was no doubt due to immigration into the area. In addition, a relocation of the existing settlements took place. This phenomenon is explicitly referred to by Watters (1971) for shifting cultivators in Venezuela and by Ward (1968) for the more stable pattern of settlement characteristic of New Guinea. In the mid 1960s, the present author saw tangible evidence of this process in the form of newly established compounds along recently opened roads in Nigeria.

In many parts of the world, the transport network has evolved beyond the simple pattern with which we have been concerned so far, but not to the point at which all settlements are fully connected to the national road network. Under these circumstances, a much more complex pattern of land use and development will occur, but nevertheless one in which accessibility to transport will be an identifiable factor of importance. India is a striking case in question. Table 11 shows the percentage distribution of the estimated 570,000 rural villages, arranged by distance from an all-weather road. As Owen (1968, 52) comments: 'Very few Indian farmers more than a mile or a mile and a half [1.6–2.4 km] from a reasonably good road are using modern methods,' by which he means not only modern seeds, fertilizers, etc., with implications for the intensity of land use, but also the kinds of crops and the extent to which they are marketed. The importance of accessibility is also evident from the factor-analytic study of 108 Indian villages conducted by Adelman and Dalton

Table 11 *India, 1959: percentage distribution of villages by distance from an all-weather road*

Distance (km)	Percentage of villages
within village	10.9
up to 2.4	18.2
2.4–5.6	20.7
5.6–8.9	12.3
8.9–16.9	15.9
16.9–32.2	9.6
over 32.2	7.8
information not available	4.6
	100.0

Source: Owen 1968, 52

(1971). This essentially descriptive technique showed that 36 per cent of the variance in accessibility is associated with the economic and modernization factor which they identified; accessibility is also associated with the extent to which agriculture dominates the local economy.

A final comment will serve to conclude this section. The reality of the phenomena that have been discussed in this section is so striking that it has become commonplace to incorporate them in formal evaluations of investment projects (e.g. Wilson *et al.* 1966). Although the technique of benefit–cost analysis is fraught with difficulty, the scale of investment projects and the involvement of national and international organizations require that some form of 'accountancy' be employed. One of the very early studies, and certainly one of the most thorough, to employ an agricultural location model to aid the appraisal of transport investment was published by Bourrières in 1950. As an engineer, he appears to have been unfamiliar with von Thünen's ideas. Bourrières developed his analysis from the conditions prevailing in the Ivory Coast in the late 1930s and early 1940s. The whole economy was then based upon the export of a limited range of primary products such as cotton, palm oil and timber, which were evacuated by a single railway running inland from Abidjan, supplemented by a rudimentary network of roads. Foodstuffs were grown for local consumption but other material needs were supplied by imports.

For practical purposes, Bourrières was able to assume that prices at Abidjan were fixed, determined by the state of the world market and not to be influenced by the Ivory Coast. He possessed data on transport costs and costs of production for the various crops, which enabled him to estimate the expected extent and disposition of production zones in relation to proposals for improving communications. These production data then provided the information necessary to determine the expected level of government revenues, which could be set against the cost incurred in providing better transport facilities. By these means, he arrived at proposals for improvements and was able to show that they would be advantageous, especially in the forested southern area, which was then already the most developed.

United Kingdom

In considering the more complicated regional and world patterns, it is helpful to direct attention in some detail to a particular case, and then to show that what is true in one instance also holds more generally. For this purpose, the United Kingdom has been chosen.

We shall begin with a brief study of the development of land use around the city of London up to the advent of the railways, go on to discuss the horticultural and dairying industries during the nineteenth and twentieth centuries and then examine some aspects of the evolution and contemporary structure of imports. This will bring the account up to approximately 1973, in which year Britain joined the European Economic Community.

The story may begin with the century 1540–1640, which has been documented by Fisher (1934–5; see also Thirsk 1967). At the end of the sixteenth century, London's food supplies came almost exclusively from a few adjoining shires. 'But as the years pass it is possible to watch the city's tentacles spreading over the provinces until by the middle of the seventeenth century they reached to Berwick, Cornwall and Wales.' Kent was the great granary of London early in the period, but to an increasing extent fruit and vegetable cultivation invaded this and other areas bordering the city, while grain supplies were drawn from further afield, notably Norfolk. (Interestingly enough, the production of fresh fruit in Kent represented an innovation in the reign of Elizabeth I, replacing imports from the Low Countries.) While fresh milk and fresh butter were local produce, cheese and salted butter were increasingly brought from further than Essex and Suffolk, from as far as Durham and Northumberland. The meat trade was organized on a national basis, animals and birds being driven from Wales or the north-west of England, pausing in the hither regions to be fattened for market.

The position outlined above was reflected in the prices for grain (Table 12). Although prices were clearly affected by local and regional supply and demand factors, the higher London prices are striking. Defoe (1948), writing in the first quarter of the eighteenth century, drew attention to the same phenomenon. Note also that agricultural wages within 32 kilometres of London were higher by about 75 per cent than in areas distant 177 kilometres or more (Gilboy 1934).

Table 12 *England: decennial average prices of wheat, shillings per quarter*

	1540–9	1640–9
London	6.88	49.91
Exeter	6.44	44.95
Oxford	4.63	42.53
Winchester	5.24	38.75
Cambridge	4.70	36.76

Source: Thirsk 1967

The general pattern of agriculture and related land use dependent upon London remained essentially intact until the time of the Napoleonic wars and later. However, by about 1750 a well-articulated national grain market had become established, in which London prices were not necessarily higher than elsewhere (Granger and Elliott 1967). Also, with the growth of the coalfield industrial areas in the nineteenth century, agricultural wages elsewhere rose above those paid in the vicinity of the Metropolis (Hunt 1973). Other important changes occurred during that century and subsequently, notably the increased consumption of liquid milk.

As even a cursory glance will show, the environs of London comprehend a wide range of natural soil conditions, ranging from intractable clays in Essex and Middlesex to light and fertile loams on some of the river gravels, to poor but easily worked land on the exposed chalk. Despite this wide variety, the Reverend Henry Hunter, writing in 1811, 'described the face of the land around the capital in terms of a series of concentric belts, each displaying a measure of unity of farming practice' (Bull 1956, 28; see also East 1937). Beyond the area of buildings and circumadjacent clay pits, a zone of pasture extended to a distance of several kilometres to the north and further in other directions, especially to the west. This pasture was almost exclusively in the hands of cow-keepers; in addition, even early in the century much milk was produced in town dairies, to which fodder was carried over distances of 30 to 40 km (Atkins 1977*a* and 1977*b*). At this period, dung was being transported up to 30 km by cart and even further by barge (Morgan 1973), for use in horticulture as well as on the pastures. Beyond the pasture and hay lands, arable farming with leys of clover and grass became the dominant form of agricultural enterprise. Cutting across these belts was a strip of market gardens extending westwards along the Thames gravels: in this case there was generally a close association between the nature of the soil and the type of enterprise, although this form of production was not confined to the lands best suited to it, but was also found, for example, on the heavier lands to the north-east. As with the pasture and hither hay land, the horticultural holdings received plentiful inputs of manure carted from the city.

The reasons for this pattern are not far to seek. London represented a sizeable market for agricultural produce; communications were not good, with the consequence that carrying foodstuffs more than a few kilometres took much time; and certain kinds of produce were highly perishable. By themselves, these considerations were sufficient to ensure that if Londoners were going to consume any quantities of fresh milk and any of a wide range of fresh fruits and vegetables, these would have to be local produce, coming from as near the capital as possible. But in addition, transport provision within the city depended upon horses, and the fodder, particularly the hay, was too bulky to be transported far overland. The population of horses and stall-fed cattle gave a plentiful supply of street sweepings and manure which had to be removed but which was not worth carting very far. The less perishable foods, such as grain, which were reasonably valuable in relation to their bulk could withstand the cost of transport over considerable distances and were perforce banished from the nearer lands. Livestock were walked to market from as far as Wales, the Pennines and even Scotland; they lost condition on the way, but this was often restored by a short period for fattening somewhere in the Home Counties. Notice, also, that the zones of supply extended further along the east coast than elsewhere, on account of the relatively easy access by sea.

With the development of the railways and refrigeration during the last century, and of road transport and pasteurization in this, the distance over which milk may be transported and remain in good condition has increased from mere tens of kilometres to hundreds. This has made possible a great enlargement in the area supplying fresh milk to the urban markets. That such an increase has in fact taken place may be attributed to a variety of factors. The urban population has grown a great deal and with rising living standards the *per caput* consumption of milk has also increased, the combined effect being to raise demand manifold. Cattle disease in the town dairies of London in the 1860s and licensing of such establishments rendered them less attractive propositions than hitherto, while towards the end of the century the growing import of grain struck a heavy blow at arable farming. Much arable land was turned to pasture to supply the rising demand for liquid milk. At the same time, imports of meat and dairy produce forced many farmers away from the production of butter and cheese to the more lucrative business of fresh milk. So radical has been the transformation of British agriculture as a consequence of these forces that currently about a quarter of the gross farm income derives from milk and milk products (mostly liquid milk). Furthermore, most of the country lies within the supply areas of the major urban concentrations: the zone of liquid milk production has extended to embrace almost the whole country (Whetham 1964 and 1970).

Prior to the 1930s, the market for milk was not regulated, so that producers of liquid milk located near the main urban markets were at an advantage relative to more distant dairy farmers. Thus, in the period 1906–14, transport costs amounted to 27 per cent of the farm-gate price for producers situated more than 160 km from their market (Coppock 1971). The average market realization for milk in June 1934 in the south-west peninsula was only 63 per cent of the price obtained in the south-east (Baker 1973), a price differential that was reflected in the proportion of milk used for manufacturing as compared with liquid consumption. However, in 1933 the Milk Marketing Board was established and within a few years organized a regulated market in which regional price differences were almost entirely obliterated. Although Rayner (1975) concludes that with the rapid reduction in the relative cost of transport the element of regional cross-subsidization is now small (a 'tax' on south-east producers of only six per cent of average producer prices), many producers in the south-east would like greater regional variation in prices; their case was argued by Whetstone (1970), but has been rejected.

As to horticulture, a glance at a land-use map of this country will show at once that there is a marked concentration of market gardening into certain areas of the country. Broadly speaking, the areas may be divided into those which are situated adjacent to major urban areas and those which are located where natural conditions of soil and climate are peculiarly favourable. Middlesex, Bedfordshire and Lancashire, for example, contain much horticulture which comes in the former category, and Lincolnshire and Cornwall that which falls within the latter. Stated in these terms, where indeed is the influence of distance?

To answer this question, it is necessary to have a closer look at the individual crops, for fruits and vegetables are very diverse in their characteristics and requirements. There is the important antithesis between maincrop products with a long selling season which command relatively low prices per unit weight and usually also per hectare, such as turnips and cabbages, and speciality crops with a limited season which fetch high prices, examples being early potatoes and asparagus. Then there is also the contrast between the highly perishable crops and those which remain in good condition for considerable periods after harvesting; lettuces are a case of the former, lasting barely a few hours after cutting, and onions illustrate the latter case, keeping for months. Each separate crop has its own unique combination of characteristics and therefore analysis of spatial distributions must be concerned with particular products.

The two broad locational categories of fruit and vegetable growing mentioned above concentrate on different kinds of produce which are grown in a different manner. Near the cities, market gardeners still cultivate the more valuable and perishable crops, such as salad onions and runner beans, in an intensive manner on comparatively small holdings. In the case of lettuce, there is little doubt that the

growing areas are so situated in relation to the consuming areas that only for the produce of about one-third of the area grown in England and Wales have markets to be found at distances further than approximately 20 miles [32 kilometres]. [Ministry of Agriculture, Fisheries and Food 1967, 44]

With lettuce and similar crops, grown either in the open or under glass, the greater part of production is located within one hour's journey time of the main urban centres. In contrast, the cheaper, bulky vegetables, such as parsnips and potatoes, are mostly grown as part of an arable rotation. The individual farmer normally specializes in a few of these crops and grows each on a substantial scale. The intensity of cultivation is lower than on the market gardens and though the crop is of comparatively low value it does not deteriorate quickly and can be handled in large consignments. Hence, crops like carrots or celery may be highly localized in the arable districts – mainly in eastern England – where soils and terrain are suitable.

Nevertheless, these crops are all grown within a day's journey of the market.

Table 13 reflects these various considerations as they apply to eighteen crops that can be compared for the years 1956 and 1973. With the reform of local government that became operative in April 1974, county boundaries were changed and comparison with later years is impossible. The coefficient of localization is the same as that devised by Florence (1944) for the analysis of industrial location, except that the area planted to the respective crops has been used instead of employed persons. The coefficient is obtained by computing the percentage of the total area in each crop in England and Wales found in each county. These percentages are compared with the percentage distribution among the counties of the aggregate area of the specified crops. For example, 20.13 per cent of the area under Brussels sprouts in 1973 was in Bedfordshire, whereas that county contained only 3.47 per cent of the total area under the eighteen crops. This is a positive deviation of 16.66 per cent. All the positive deviations are summed for the crop in question and the resulting aggregate is divided by 100. If a particular crop were distributed among the counties in a manner identical to the average, the coefficient of localization would be zero. At the other extreme, a value approaching unity indicates a very high degree of localization with respect to the average of the crops. The actual degree of localization is often greater than indicated, for it frequently happens that a very small locality within the county contains that county's total area of the particular crop, or that the localized production area straddles one or more county boundaries. Coppock (1971) notes that in 1961 75 per cent of celery production was within 32 km of Littleport, Cambridgeshire, and over 50 per cent of Brussels sprouts within 24 km of Biggleswade in Bedfordshire; in both cases these radii include parts of adjoining counties.

The table indicates a slight tendency for the degree of localization to increase over time, the median coefficient having risen from 0.39 to 0.42. However, calculating the weighted coefficient, using the planted areas as weights, the coefficient fell slightly, from 0.37 to 0.36. On the other hand, the localization of the *total* area planted to the eighteen crops relative to farming as a whole increased dramatically, the relevant coefficient being 0.37 in 1956 and 0.43 in 1973. The counties with the outstanding increases in relative concentration of horticulture were the Holland and Lindsey divisions of Lincolnshire,

Table 13 *England and Wales, 1956 and 1973: the localization of open-air horticultural production based on acreage returns*

Crop	Coefficient of localization		Total area (thousand hectares)	
	1956	1973	1956	1973
runner and French beans	0.37	0.25	5.0	12.2
broad beans	0.31	0.29	3.2	4.4
peas, green for canning and freezing	0.32	0.32	19.4	50.4
peas, harvested dry	0.39	0.32	42.5	21.7
onions	0.26	0.32	2.3	6.5
Brussels sprouts	0.46	0.33	19.5	15.6
beetroot	0.28	0.35	3.8	3.1
cabbages, savoys, kale, cauliflower, broccoli	0.24	0.38	32.3	28.4
strawberries	0.39	0.39	6.8	6.7
lettuce	0.41	0.45	3.1	4.7
peas, green for marketing	0.45	0.47	14.7	4.7
carrots	0.42	0.48	13.1	13.3
parsnips	0.31	0.48	2.0	2.3
gooseberries	0.43	0.49	2.3	1.2
celery	0.60	0.52	1.9	1.8
blackcurrants	0.44	0.54	4.2	3.8
turnips and swedes	0.35	0.54	2.2	2.5
raspberries	0.48	0.56	1.1	0.8
			179.4	184.2

Source: Ministry of Agriculture, *Agricultural Statistics, England and Wales*

and Norfolk; collectively, they accounted for 27 per cent of the area in the eighteen crops in the latter year.

Following the demise of town dairies in the 1860s and the development of mechanized urban transport during the nineteenth century, the availability of manure supplies from the cities had ceased to be an important location factor early in the twentieth century. On the other hand, the major urban centres continued to be the source of much casual labour, essential for the harvesting of many crops, until after the Second World War. Since then, mechanical harvesting devices – for peas, hops, sugar beet, etc. – have been steadily replacing the gangs of seasonal workers for an ever growing number of crops. *The Times* (4 September 1973) reported that only about 10,000 pickers were employed in the nation's hop farms, compared with the 100,000, mainly drawn from the East End of London, that used to engage in the urban exodus.

Cities have therefore very largely ceased to be important for the supply of two inputs, thereby facilitating the movement of many crops away from the peri-urban areas. However, problems of marketing do still affect many crops, primarily the highly perishable ones like lettuce, and also hardy nursery stock. Much of the latter is grown in scattered locations around but near the main population centres, accessible to the car-owning purchaser who wishes to inspect plants before making his choice. Postal sales on catalogue specifications have not yet seriously modified this pattern.

Other crops have been affected by changes in the manner of marketing, whereby comparatively few merchants now handle most of the sales so that continuity of supply can be ensured and economies of harvesting and selling secured.

Merchants, of whom the number is not large, usually specialize in particular crops or related crops. Chatteris in the Isle of Ely is the centre for the carrot merchants, who may also handle other vegetables such as parsnips and celery, while in the districts around Boston and Wainfleet are those whose main business is in cauliflowers and spring cabbages. . . . For the most part they are themselves substantial growers of the crops they handle. . . . To ensure continuity of supply (an essential part of their business) they may enter into financial arrangements with the smaller growers, usually by agreeing to buy their growing crops by the acre. Moreover, they invariably carry out the harvesting of the crops, having gangs of labour with special experience in this task, and for which the smaller grower is usually ill-provided. [Ministry of Agriculture, Fisheries and Food 1967, 44]

The passage quoted above has been confirmed in respect of carrots by Hinton's (1971) study of the economics of that industry, and the phenomenon is in fact general to many edible crops, including fruit, and also to flowers (Ministry of Agriculture, Fisheries and Food 1970). Where the produce is harvested for freezing, it is essential for the crop to reach the processing factory within one or two hours, which necessarily limits the supply radius very seriously indeed

(Andrews and Lilwall 1974). Since the freezing of both fruit and vegetables has developed very rapidly, this new reason for the localization of horticultural output is acquiring ever greater importance. Although the precise form of these economies of scale effects has been changing over time, the contemporary changes are recognizably similar to those described by Harvey (1963) for the Kentish hop industry in the nineteenth century.

The distribution of some crops is not as readily explained in the terms that have so far been used. The area around Bedford has long been prominent for Brussels sprouts yet the light sandy soils, especially near Sandy, are not especially suitable for this crop, and localization does not appear to have been occasioned by economies in marketing. Nor does there seem to be an adequate explanation for the concentration of rhubarb production near Leeds and of loganberries and cultivated blackberries in Worcestershire and Kent. Nevertheless, when particular crops are viewed in terms of their own characteristics and are related to farming and merchanting systems as a whole, the disorder that appeared at first sight resolves itself into a remarkably rational pattern.

Peet (1969), examined the structure of Britain's import trade during the nineteenth and early twentieth centuries; his main findings are summarized in Tables 14 and 15. The former shows that though the relative significance of imports was rising, the rank-order of products changed hardly at all, and that the more perishable and/or bulky the commodity, the greater the degree of national self-sufficiency. Table 15 further shows that although there was a dramatic expansion of the supply system, the mean distance of imports commodity by commodity shows a systematic and remarkably stable pattern which conforms with *a priori* expectations. From Peet's evidence, there can be no doubt that the spatial structure of food production and imports conformed very closely with theory in the nineteenth century and up to the First World War.

Earlier editions of this book reported evidence showing that a systematic spatial arrangement of production and imports was apparent in the 1960s (Chisholm 1968). In view of the information provided by Peet, it is clearly not necessary to rehearse that evidence at length. Suffice it to say that the patterns of production and import for fruits, vegetables, dairy products and meat remain virtually undisturbed, providing well over a century of continuity.

There is a great deal more that could be said about British agricul-

Table 14 *United Kingdom: imports as a percentage of apparent consumption*

Commodity group	1870–6	1904–10
milk	0	0.1
fruit and vegetables	8	24
meat and livestock	12	36
dairy and poultry products (except milk)	40	53
feed grains	39	61
wheat and flour	50	84
wool	53	80
all above commodities	26	46

Source: Peet 1969

Table 15 *Average distances from London to regions from which imports were obtained* (km)*

Import type	1831–35	1856–60	1871–75	1891–95	1909–13
fruit and vegetables	0†	520	860	1850	3020
live animals	0†	1010	1400	3680	7240
butter, cheese, eggs, etc.	420	850	2160	2590	5020
feed grains	1380	3270	3910	5210	7770
flax and seeds	2450	5230	4460	6560	6280
meat and tallow	3220	4670	6020	8130	10 060
wheat and flour	3910	3490	6760	8290	9570
wool and hides	3750	14 210	16 090	17 720	17 540
weighted average all above imports	2930	5870	6920	8130	9460

* 'Imports' from Ireland not included.
† No significant imports.

Source: Peet 1969

ture in relation to imports, to show how, at appropriate levels of disaggregation, location patterns do conform to theory. It will be sufficient to make just two further points. The first concerns grain production. One of the important things to notice is that the yields of grain crops in this country, in common with north-west Europe, are much higher than in the countries which provide the main export supplies. Two reasons may be adduced. The first is that climatic and soil conditions in Britain and Europe are more suitable for heavy yields than are those found in Argentina, Australia and elsewhere. Second, that in this island and neighbouring countries there is a multitude of products which may profitably be produced, whereas in the arid plains which are far removed from markets the alternatives are minimal. If grains are going to be produced at all in this country, intensive production is imperative because other crops are readily available and eagerly compete for the farmers' attention.

Furthermore, one must note that the greater part of grain output is used for animal feed, either on the farm of origin or elsewhere. Indeed, so important a feature of Britain's grain economy has this become that, writing in 1969, Britton placed the section on animal feeding-stuffs before his treatment of human consumption, malting and manufacturing. Thus, grain production in Britain may truly be regarded as an integral part of the meat and dairy enterprises and consequently reflects, albeit indirectly, the advantages of proximity to market.

The second point, which applies primarily, but not exclusively, to fruit and vegetables, is the seasonality of imports. For example, of all fruit imports, 68 per cent enter the United Kingdom in the period February to August, when home supplies (berry fruits excepted) are at their lowest (Kirk and Ellis 1971). Furthermore, the spatial pattern of imports is itself a reflection of the combined effect of the differential march of the seasons in various regions and the minimization of transport costs, among other considerations. The matter is well illustrated by the case of potatoes. In a normal year, the production of maincrop varieties suffices for virtually all our ware potato requirements with but small supplementary imports, mainly from Belgium and the Netherlands. But home-produced new potatoes do not begin to come on to the market until the year is well advanced; especially in the months of May and June the gap is filled by imports. Table 16 sets out the relevant information for 1962. It will be seen at once that the eleven countries listed may be separated into three major divisions: the Canary Islands and Morocco have a clear advantage in the early months of the year, Belgium and the Netherlands in July. The pattern of exports from the remaining countries is less clear-cut. The greater period over which these countries send their major contributions may be due to the variety of physical conditions found within their borders, which attribute is particularly striking for Italy. Indeed, Italy clearly displays within her own confines the principle which underlies the seasonal distribution of the sources of our new potato imports: as the season advances, the demand for supplies can be met by lands lying progressively further north and nearer the destination of the consignments. Like a concertina, the supply area expands and contracts, according to the season.

Table 16 *United Kingdom, 1962: imports of new potatoes February–July (percentage of imports, by weight)*

Country of origin	February	March	April	May	June	July
Belgium	—	—	—	0.5	0.5	16.7
Greece	—	—	—	3.9	4.2	7.7
Egypt	—	2.8	2.1	11.7	1.4	16.3
France	—	—	—	0.2	6.5	0.2
Netherlands	—	—	—	5.0	6.0	3.0
Cyprus	24.6	14.2	2.9	10.6	40.4	16.4
Italy	2.3	0.3	5.1	13.1	31.1	11.9
Malta and Gozo	—	—	1.5	2.9	0.6	—
Spain	1.3	21.0	37.4	39.9	—	—
Canary Is.	22.3	27.2	37.5	5.9	0.7	—
Morocco	49.5	29.8	12.7	0.7	1.6	0.5
others	—	4.7	0.8	5.6	7.0	27.3
total	100.0	100.0	100.0	100.0	100.0	100.00
Total imports, tonnes	11 360	36 340	37 000	113 710	120 150	41 050

Source: Potato Marketing Board, *Report on the Operation of the Potato Marketing Scheme,* year ended 30 June 1962 (1962 is the last year for which the Board published these data)

Enough has been said about British agriculture, both in its evolution and also as it is in contemporary times, to show both the long-term stability in the pattern of production plus imports, and the impress of distance constraints. Clearly, although formal agricultural location theory supplies only part of the explanation of observed patterns, that part is both important and indispensable, alike in historical times and the present day.

Other cases

In this concluding section, we will briefly review evidence relating to land-use zoning around individual cities and at the wider regional and inter-regional scale. At both scales, it is relevant to cite both contemporary and historical cases.

Hamburg is the main centre of consumption in northern Germany. Using 1950 production and crop-area data by the smallest German administrative unit, the *Gemeinde*, and plotting distributions by units of 10 hectares, Stamer (1952) showed that an irregular concentric zoning of land uses obtains. The fundamental factor causing this he found to be distance from Hamburg, with modifications to the ideal pattern arising from conditions of the physical environment. His findings are summarized below:

Zone 1 city
allotments

Zone 2 commercial horticulture   irregular distribution in this inner
fruit   zone on account of differing soil
osiers   conditions
nurseries

Zone 3 arable farming   cattle to the west – lowland
cattle farming   arable to the east – better-drained land

Hurwitz examined the development of agriculture in Natal and came to the conclusion that

A striking feature of this study has been the development of the major production zones in conformity with land-use theory. Land use can be explained by the principle of comparative advantage. . . . [Hurwitz 1957, 106]

He enumerated physical and social factors, but laid stress on von Thünen's ideas as the dominant consideration, zones of land use centring on Durban and cutting across physical boundaries. Indeed, Africa supplies us with many examples of cities surrounded by recognizable annuli, associated with the supply of staple foodstuffs. Those in tropical West Africa draw most of their food from within distances that rarely exceed 80 or 160 km (Johnson 1958), though elsewhere in the continent the limiting distance is somewhat greater – 282 km for Nairobi and 201 km in the case of Freetown (Jones 1972), and up to 241 km for Kampala (Oloya and Poleman 1969).

The largest city in tropical Africa is Ibadan (population in the order of one million), a city which has been particularly well documented (Akinola 1964; Güsten 1968; Oluwasanmi 1967). The total quantity supplied per square kilometre *per annum* declines with distance from the city, in the manner that might be expected. Within this aggregate picture, the spatial pattern is affected by climatic considerations as well as the cost of transport. Onions, for example, are supplied from the drier northern zone. On the other hand, fresh fruit and vegetables, as well as bulky yams, are supplied locally, while gari (a flour made from cassava) comes from far afield and especially the east. Most of the 600 tonnes of staple foodstuffs required daily arrives by lorry and mammy-wagon, but almost 3 per cent by weight is carried as head loads by women who walk up to 8 kilometres to market. These head-loaded goods are the lighter, more valuable and often perishable goods, including oranges and vegetables.

Tokyo receives most of its supply of fresh vegetables from distances less than 42 km (Eyre 1959), and Singapore still has a substantial urban dairy industry which is directly analogous to that which used to exist in London and other urban centres in both Europe and North America (Wikkramatileke and Singh 1970). Finally, contemporary Kano, in Northern Nigeria, is a source of manure for the surrounding agricultural land. This manure is carried in panniers by donkeys up to 6 kilometres, providing an essential ingredient of the intensive farming that characterizes the areas around the city (Mortimore and Wilson 1965).

The continuity of development over many centuries, with the steady expansion of food supply zones, has been carefully documented for the grain trade of France (Usher 1913) and for Paris in particular (Phlipponneau 1956). From the end of the fourteenth century to the present day, enterprises such as fruit and vegetable production, cut flowers and nurseries have clung to the skirts of the French capital. The less intensive forms of agriculture, arable farming and stock raising, have occupied more distant lands. Within western Europe as a whole, from Italy to Cologne, all the major cities in the twelfth century possessed a zone of suburban agriculture, wherein vegetables and vineyards were common elements (Koebner 1966). This suburban agriculture was often associated with the holding of land by town-dwellers; in cities such as Orvieto and Perugia, approximately two-thirds of the townsmen held land late in the thirteenth century (Jones 1966). Overland supplies of grain to Florence, early in the sixteenth century, were brought by wagon and pack-horse for no more than 19 km (Parry 1967). Such a limited radius may seem surprising but even in the eighteenth century Cantillon took it for granted that food would not normally be transported more than 15 km from its place of origin (Clark and Haswell 1970). On the other hand, overland transport in mid-fourteenth-century England added only 15 per cent to the cost of grain if the journey were 80 km (Postan 1952).

Associated with this pattern of food supplies for cities was a general problem of removing ordure and night-soil from the built-up areas. There was certainly an organized trade in this urban manure, in the case of Antwerp as early as the sixteenth century, and: 'By the mid seventeenth century most cities [in Holland] had franchised men to collect refuse and sell and deliver it to farmers' (de Vries 1974, 150).

Outside Europe, it is interesting to note how the principles described above have been used as a framework in which to write the history of Spanish dominion in Middle America (Ewald 1977; West and Augelli 1966). With the development of gold and silver mines in northern Mexico, and urban centres throughout the Spanish dominions, discrete localized markets for agricultural supplies grew up, each monopolistically supplied from within a 'very circumscribed circle in its immediate vicinity' (Brading 1971, 16). Given the highly variable terrain and the evolution of the main communications network, the supply zones were neither necessarily contiguous to the market nor concentric in their disposition, but nevertheless conformed to the general pattern suggested by agricultural location theory.

Turning to a larger geographical scale in modern times, one of the more thorough studies of the agricultural regions of Europe remains that published by Jonasson in 1925 and 1926. After an exposition of some of von Thünen's ideas, he characterized western Europe in the following terms:

Northwest Europe may be regarded as one vast conurbation, and considered as one geographic center of consumption and market facilities for the agricultural products of the entire inner belt of horticulture, olericulture, dairying and other intensive land uses. . . . [Jonasson 1925, 289–90]

The point is confirmed by a map which van Valkenburg and Held (1952) have prepared showing that the average yield of eight crops declines with increasing distance from the area of most intensive farming centred on the Low Countries, Denmark and south-east

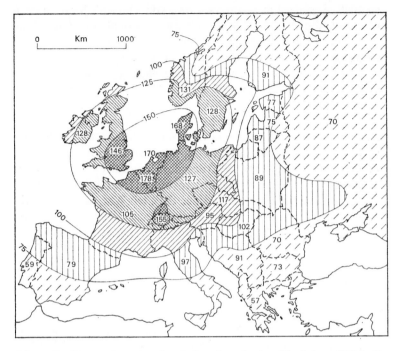

Figure 5 *Europe: intensity of agricultural production. The index of 100 is the average European yield per acre of eight main crops: wheat, rye, barley, oats, corn, potatoes, sugar beet and hay. 1937 political boundaries.* Source: van Valkenburg and Held 1952

England (see Figure 5). The regularity of the decline in yields is astonishing. Several scholars have noted that the agriculture of the United States displays spatial regularities very similar to those evident in Europe. Watson (1963) compiled a map of part of the United States, extending about 1600 km around Chicago, a city that acts as a major food processing and trans-shipping centre. The predominant land uses were intensive dairy and truck farming near Chicago, followed by cattle and swine fattening, extensive wheat farming, and cattle rearing, located at greater distances. Other scholars have examined aspects of agriculture for the entire United States. Jones (1976) found that grain production, when viewed dichotomously as wheat for human consumption and feed grain for livestock, is

spatially organized in accordance with von Thünen's location principles; the food wheat is produced in the western plains, remote from
the main markets, and the feed grains in the mid-west and east
(compare page 84). Net farm income is a measure of the overall
intensity of production. With data available by counties, Muller
(1973) fitted various forms of trend surface; his preferred version
is the quartic surface, reproduced here as Figure 6, showing three
focal points for high net incomes – the north-eastern seaboard, Florida
and California – and yielding a value for R^2 of 0.47. Given the wide
variety of environmental conditions, this is an impressively good fit.
Finally, Jumper (1969 and 1974) describes how dairy farming and the
production of fruit and vegetables have moved from their immediately
peri-urban locations, especially since the Civil War, and how in the
present day the seasonal pattern of vegetable supplies conforms to the
principle illustrated by the import of new potatoes into the United
Kingdom (page 84).

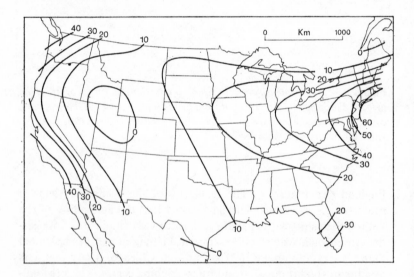

Figure 6   *United States: net farm income per acre. Quartic trend surface,*
$10 contour interval. Source: Muller 1973

Zoning of agricultural production within nations has been reported
by numerous workers in all parts of the world, and only a few examples will be quoted. Kayser and Tricart (1957) prepared maps of

groundnut production in Senegal for three separate years – 1900, 1937 and 1950 – identifying areas of considerable, medium and slight production. Groundnuts are a cash crop, the greater part of production being exported. In each year, the zone of most intensive production lay near the coast, the area of sparse output inland, where transport was more difficult and costly. Whereas in 1900 cultivation ceased at about 200 kilometres from Dakar, by 1950 the limit was 600 kilometres and the area of considerable yield had extended over regions of moderate output, which in turn had encroached on localities where formerly production was scanty or non-existent. Griffin (1973) has shown that Montevideo acts as the 'central city' for the entire agricultural sector in Uruguay, while Scott concluded that Australia's agriculture displays intermingled zoning about several main urban centres:

The basic zonation of rural land use oriented to the metropolitan areas in Australia may be stated as a sequence outward from the city of crop farming, dairying, livestock fattening, wheat-sheep farming, sheep grazing, and cattle grazing. An additional type of perhaps basic importance is intensive cropping located by factors other than metropolitan dominance. [Scott 1968, 244]

If a nation or region is small (in economic terms) and has no major urban centre of its own, then its agricultural economy must be interpreted in terms of the world economy. Thus, Brookfield and Hart (1971) found it relevant to consider the Pacific islands as part of von Thünen's outermost ring. The staple exports are goods that have experienced a large reduction in volume from the raw state: milled sugar 13 per cent of the weight of cane; coffee beans 15 per cent of the weight of the cherry; good quality copra 14–20 per cent of the weight of unhusked nut. Indeed, to illustrate their argument, they compiled a world map identifying four trade 'rings' which represent an inversion of the traditional von Thünen system (see Figure 7). Ring I is the world's outermost ring, while Ring IV is the 'world central city' around the North Atlantic basin.

Historians have recognized the importance of agricultural location theory as a framework within which to analyse the unfolding panorama of the past. Explicitly referring to von Thünen's ideas, and their relevance to conditions in the past, Schlebecker (1960) went on to describe western Europe and the eastern United States as one metropolitan area in the world context. With the expansion of

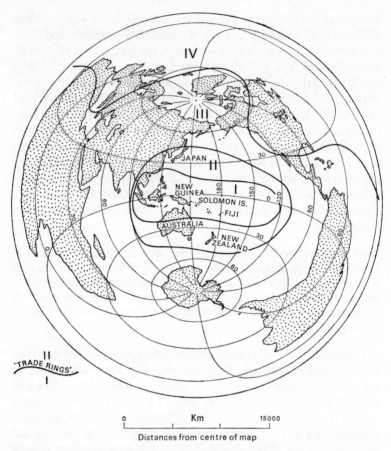

Figure 7 *Melanesia and its trade rings*. Source: Brookfield and Hart 1971

demand in this 'metropolis' and the improvement of transport facilities
during the nineteenth century (allied to the peopling of the prairies),
he noted that any one area experienced a succession of land uses
which, in their temporal sequence, matched the outward expansion
of supply zones. An altogether more important study by an historian
is Wallerstein's (1974) examination of the development and articula-
tion of the world economy in the sixteenth century, focused on
Europe and including what the author called the 'periphery' and the
'external arena'; however, Wallerstein makes no reference to the
corpus of literature cited in the present book and it appears that he

came to his ideas by an independent route. Aspects of European history can be the better understood when it is realized that between 1500 and 1650 the population of what is now the Netherlands doubled, while similar developments were occurring in Germany. Food supply zones were substantially extended; cattle were driven from northern Jutland to Zealand, while grain supplies from the Baltic and Poland became of vital importance. This process has been carefully documented by Glamann (1971 and 1977), while de Vries (1974) provides ample evidence on the manner in which Dutch agriculture was intensified *circa* 1550 to *circa* 1650. Grigg (1974) has supplemented the account of agricultural changes in northern Europe with a description of the evolution of production and trade in the Mediterranean basin, in which the combination of rising demand and technical change led to expansion of the supply zones for wine, olive oil, fruit and vegetables. Finally, the historical process in Europe has been discussed in explicitly Thünian terms by Peet (1970–71 and 1972).

Whether attention is directed to contemporary or historical cases, the last few paragraphs have in fact been dealing with aspects of international location of production and trade. Thus have we come to a subject that has attracted many eminent scholars. Formal explanations for the existence of, and benefits derived from, international trade build upon the fundamental notion of comparative advantage. As Ohlin noted in his classic study *Interregional and International Trade* (1933, 142): 'international trade theory cannot be understood except in relation to and as a part of general localization theory'.

5 The analysis inverted

The examination in the last two chapters of the land-use patterns which develop round settlements has been based on the assumption that the location of the settlement or major concentration of population is given and fixed. But is not much of the zoning of types and intensities of land uses, which we have ascribed to distance, in reality due to conditions of the physical environment? For example, is it not the case that often the poorer soils are reserved for grazing, these soils being situated away from the village, while the better soils which are more suited to arable cultivation are found nearer at hand? Or that the interior of Australia is much drier and more impoverished than the littoral regions where the main population centres are found, which means there is inevitably a systematic arrangement of land uses so that the intensity of use falls as one moves further away from the main markets? There is indeed much truth in this objection. At first sight, this admission may seem to limit the validity of the case to those circumstances in which the physical conditions of climate, soil, relief, etc., are approximately uniform over the area in question. But this is not so. If we cease to assume that the location of settlements is predetermined, then the principles which have been described can be inverted: if natural conditions and therefore land uses are taken as given, then the location of the settlements may be regarded as variable.

This chapter seeks to elaborate this other aspect of location analysis to prepare the way for Chapter 6 and Chapter 7. To simplify exposition, the argument is related to the location of villages and farmsteads, which has the additional advantage of introducing the next chapter; but the principle is of general application, as will be shown in Chapter 7.

Relations of a village to the resources exploited

To begin with a simplified example, we may imagine the establishment of a new agricultural settlement in an area of country not previously inhabited. Such a settlement has two sets of space-relationships of the utmost importance: one is the relationship to its lands
and the other is its links with the outside world – lines of communication and other inhabited centres. It will be convenient to treat
these two sets of considerations separately, dealing first with the
relationship of the settlement to the resources of its territory.

Let us imagine a people of modest cultural achievements, such as
the Anglo-Saxon colonists who settled widely over England. Such
people, in seeking places in which to build their abodes, would have
had to bear in mind the availability of arable and grazing lands, the
supply of water for man and beast, fuel resources and the ease of
obtaining building materials. In addition, there would be special
local considerations, such as defence, the need to avoid lands liable
to flooding and the ravages of malaria. But for the moment these
latter may be ignored, attention being concentrated upon the universal economic needs of an agricultural community.

Figure 8 shows the five basic elements of such a settler community's
economy: with none can the settlement dispense. As we have already
seen, the disadvantages posed by distance in conducting various
enterprises are very variable and in the figure some hypothetical
values have been assigned for each element showing the relative
disadvantage of distance. These may be thought of as units of cost
to the community; for example, the removal of water 1 kilometre is
equivalent to 10 units of cost, whereas if the source of building
materials is that far away it represents only one-tenth of the cost. It
is not particularly important for the present purpose to discuss what
the precise relative costs are, if only because they are in fact very
variable both in space and time. Water has been given a high value
on account of its traditional importance: it has to be used at frequent
intervals in the day and is difficult to carry and store in large quantities when only elementary implements are available, such as pitchers
and gourds. Arable land is usually more greedy of labour than grass-
land, requiring more cultivation and more transport of goods to and
fro, while in the traditional rural economy over much of Europe,
grazing and fuel were closely associated, both being found on the
commons. Finally, building materials have been given the least weight

because, though they are bulky and awkward to handle, they are required only at spasmodic intervals.

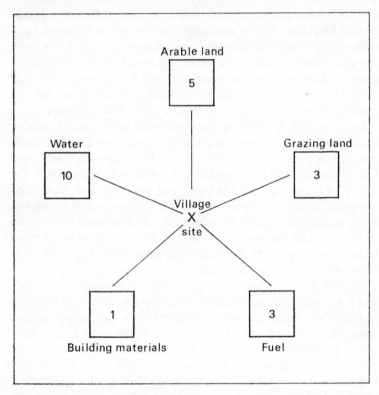

Figure 8   *Village location*

The manner in which these relationships operate can best be described by considering two hypothetical village locations, x and y, which are alternatives the one to the other. A survey of the two situations might show that the various resources were situated at distances from the spot where the village would be built as indicated in Table 17. Column D shows the cost of exploiting a particular kind of resource at the given distance of so many kilometres from the proposed village site. Location y has the smallest sum of such costs, despite that fact of being well removed from water; there would be a clear advantage in choosing it in preference to x.

Table 17 *Two hypothetical village locations*

A	B		C	D	
	Distance from village (km)		Units of cost per km from village	Product of B × C	
Resource	x	y		x	y
water	0.1	0.5	10	1.0	5.0
arable land	2.0	1.0	5	10.0	5.0
grazing land	2.5	1.5	3	7.5	4.5
fuel	2.5	2.0	3	7.5	6.0
building materials	3.0	2.0	1	3.0	2.0
				29.0	22.5

Expressed in these terms, the analysis is identical in principle to that developed by Weber, with one reservation. He was considering manufacturing industry supplied with mineral raw materials and sending the products to urban markets. The mines, the factory and the markets could all be regarded as infinitely small points of no areal extent. Such a concept clearly does not apply in the above case, since all the resources, with the possible exception of water, are distributed widely, and only the village itself approximates to a dimensionless point. This problem may be resolved in the following fashion: consider, for example, the arable land, which may be divided into numerous plots or may in imagination be carved up into units of one hectare apiece. In considering each segment, no great error is made if we assume that all the work and produce of the segment pertains to a single point located at the centre. Thus, the total 'weight' for the arable land may be obtained as the sum of the 'weights' which properly belong to each unit area. The same device may equally well be applied to the other resources which have a wide spatial extent, and so the problem of locating a settlement with respect to the lands which are to be exploited by it can be tackled in the Weberian manner. (See Weber 1929; Hoover 1948; Smith 1971; and Haggett *et al.* 1977.)

The process of choosing a situation in which to establish one or more habitations is an exercise in least-cost location analysis, if the economic aims of the community are assumed to be given. So far as the productive objectives of the community are not immutably

R.S.A.L.U.—D

fixed, it is an exercise in maximum profit location, for energies re-
leased by the choice of an optimum location may be put to additional
productive uses.

Before we turn to evidence showing that indeed the locations of
settlements are appreciably influenced by the considerations outlined above, it is worth pausing to note the following comment by
a historian:

Yet it is one thing to recognize the constraining influence of physical
obstacles which cannot readily be surmounted in an age of simple techniques and quite another to suppose that the shape of the settlements was
always appropriate to the nature of the terrain. A geographical fatalism
which rests upon the assumption that imperfect skill is consistently applied
with perfect intelligence stands self-condemned. Ignorance, prejudice,
'historical' factors connected with the local circumstances of landowner-
ship, accidents of various kinds, and mere inertia, must all be allowed a
part in determining both the form of the settlement and the direction of
economic activity in individual cases. [Lennard 1959, 269]

Some of the first published evidence available supporting the
Weberian approach to settlement location was based on historical
studies of settlements in relation to the territories they exploited. A
classic statement is that by Orwin (1954, 24):

A study of the map in any region of hill and valley shows how parish
boundaries were defined by farming considerations. Taking extreme examples so as to demonstrate the point more clearly, it may be shown how
the need for shelter, for water, for grazing-land and land for tillage, in the
proportions necessary to sustain the community, determined the size and
shape of the allocation of land which came, ultimately, to form the parish.

Orwin then proceeds to examine two areas in detail, parts of Berkshire and Lincolnshire, showing how the elongation of the parishes
in relation to the siting of the villages along the scarp foot enabled
each community economically to command the full range of local
resources, the wet grasslands of the lowland, the light ploughland at
the scarp foot and the downland grazing above. These are particularly obvious cases, but the principle has wide application:

The principles which actuated these early [Saxon] cultivators in the organization of their townships and farms were economic and technical, and
they were everywhere observed, in all the farming districts of England,
even though often less obviously. [Orwin 1954, 27]

The same point has been made by East (1956, 98) with respect to settlements in Europe:

The several types of land, distinguished on the ground of their usefulness to man, were . . . attached to a village and organised for exploitation according to certain systems and to customary practices, [and] were combined together in a certain proportion, so as best to satisfy human needs.

Archaeologists have, in recent years, recognized the implications of the above analysis for their own studies. According to Gamble (1978, 159):

The efficient exploitation of the resource packages is governed by a series of simple constraints that were first described for archaeology by Vita-Finzi and Higgs [in 1970].

In fact, though, two years previously Clarke (1968) had indicated an awareness of the significance of agricultural location theory. The Vita-Finzi and Higgs paper showed how the relative importance of archaeological sites, and the duration of their occupation, can be interpreted in terms of their location with respect to the resources exploited, the Mount Carmel area of Palestine being the study area in question. Two years later, Jarman (1972) published an explicit codification of the principles of territorial organization and settlement location in the context of archaeological studies, including case-studies (see also Clarke 1977), and soon afterwards Hammond (1974) reported on his studies of Maya settlements, using the new interpretative framework to good effect. Nevertheless, as Hodder (1977) has pointed out, serious difficulties lie in the path of the prehistorian who seeks to use locational models in too literal manner.

Historical and archaeological evidence lends itself only to inference concerning the causal mechanisms. Contemporary evidence concerning the importance of lands in the location of settlements is provided by shifting cultivators who typically move their abodes once every five to ten years (Miracle 1967). Before they were resettled in permanent abodes, the Azande always chose a very fertile strip of the soil catena, immediately above the gallery forest which marches along the valley floor. Here they found a rich sandy loam covered with a transition forest which could easily be cleared and where they could create their intensively cultivated gardens. Further afield, on the poorer sections of the catena, temporary clearances would be made for the much more extensive cultivation of millet and other crops. This position had the further advantage of providing easy access to the stream below for water. Such a location was invariably chosen in preference to any other point on the catena, even though the choice was overtly made on oracular authority. The wisdom of the oracle lay in its recognition of sound economic principles, choosing sites which minimized the efforts involved in winning a livelihood (de Schlippé 1956). Other shifting cultivators display a similar skill in choosing the site of a new abode, as in north-west Rhodesia (Trapnell and Clothier 1936), and south-east Asia (Spencer 1966). Finally, we must note the paper by Brookfield (1968) in which he explicitly analyses the location of the dwellings of shifting cultivators in relation to the 'central point' of the cultivated plots; his finding that the dwellings of the Chimbu are moved when they are more than about 1.4 km from this central point has already been mentioned (page 58).

Although he was not specifically dealing with the location choice for the settlement he studied, Nietschmann's (1973) account of the economy of the Miskito Indians on the eastern littoral of Nicaragua should be noted at this juncture. The village of Tasbapauni is situated on the coast, accessible to a variety of resources, the exploitation of which undergoes a very distinct seasonal pattern, as shown in Figure 9. Although the data do not permit a formal analysis of whether the site selected does minimize the total travel effort, the maps suggest that this is indeed the case; the need for such minimization is clear from the data in Table 2 (page 39).

A point to note in relation to the above discussion is the role of water supplies in settlement location. It is commonly noticed how settlements in Europe are generally very closely related to water sources and so it is often inferred that this 'determines' the location of villages. It should be evident, however, that water merely has a great importance relative to other requirements, which is a sufficient reason for locating near the source of supply. In the case of the scarp-foot villages found in England, such a location also happens to be the one which minimizes the costs of conducting the various enterprises found in the traditional village economy.

Under other circumstances, location with respect to water may not be so important. For the Ngwa of south-east Nigeria, 'convenience with regard to agricultural land and not the location of water is the most important factor in determining the settlement site' (Morgan

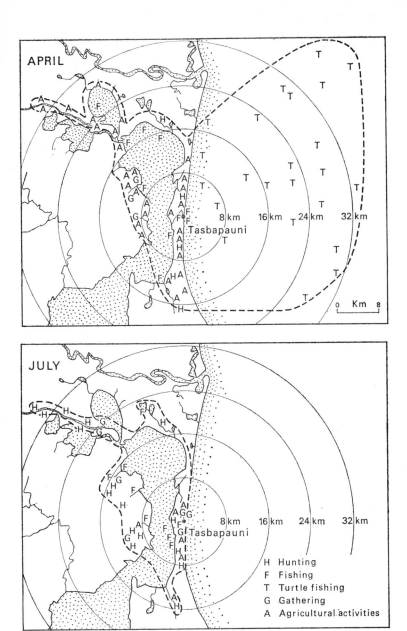

Figure 9 *Nicaragua: location of exploited food resources and associated activities, village of Tasbapauni.* Source: Nietschmann 1973

1955, 321), and the distance from permanent water may be as much as 13 kilometres. In Eastern Nigeria as a whole, about half the rural population lives more than 5 kilometres from perennial streams (Karmon 1966). Although the women and children may spend four or five hours daily in furnishing water for the household, this is mainly a dry-season task when there is comparatively little else to do, since nearby ponds supply most needs during the wet season. Evidence from East Africa (White *et al.* 1972) suggests that Eastern Nigeria may be atypical; the majority of women living in the study area scattered throughout Uganda, Tanzania and Kenya carried water less than 1.6 km. Interestingly, though, there was little variation in water use with distance of carriage up to 1.6 km but if it were necessary to go further than this, consumption *per caput* fell sharply to the barest minimum. Finally, in the Highlands of Papua-New Guinea villages are invariably located on ridges and not on the floors of the deeply incised rivers, though normally the maximum time taken to reach a source is no more than 15 minutes (Clarke 1971).

The argument of the preceding paragraphs is not impaired when we introduce considerations such as defence, the avoidance of malarial areas and avalanches. These additional requirements of a settlement site merely reduce the number of choices which are open and make the balancing of economic and non-economic advantages and disadvantages necessary. If defence is an important need, then the advantages of hill-top positions are signalled, whether Uffington Castle on Whitehorse Hill or the seven hills of Rome. But it is not any hill that will be selected – only a hill which, while meeting defence requirements, also permits the community to conduct its normal business without undue inconvenience. In practice, the best local defensive site may make life impossibly difficult owing to the separation of dwelling and cultivated land which its occupation would require, and some compromise will be adopted which reduces the military advantage somewhat but increases the economic benefit, the balance struck depending on the circumstances of time and place. Exactly the same argument applies in respect of the other additional considerations.

So far we have dealt with villages in particular, but identical considerations apply at the scale of the individual farm, using the same formulation. As with the village, the greatest weight generally attaches to the supply of water, followed by that land which is the most intensively cultivable; the terrain suitable for less intensive use can most conveniently be the furthest removed.

External relations of a settlement

But it is not sufficient to consider merely the relationship of a settlement to its lands, since only an entirely self-sufficient community has no need of regular friendly external contacts. Such communities probably no longer exist and in any case have never been particularly important, except in very remote times. Most peoples have friendly contacts of one kind or another with their neighbours and facilitating such intercourse is a cogent consideration in the choice of a location; certainly, it has become increasingly important with the passage of time, as the degree of local self-sufficiency has declined. Traditionally, the main link with other communities was through the travelling of persons and the interchange of goods, which render location on or near lines of communication an advantage. The more important these external transactions are, the greater significance attaches to access to land, river or sea routes, and the greater the advantage of a location with good external communications. The choice of a situation for a settlement would therefore depend upon a balance of considerations: the ease of conducting the internal economy of the community and the ease of concluding the external transactions. In this sense, such locations may still be viewed in terms of the Weberian system, for Weber considered both the assembly of raw materials for manufacture and the distribution of the goods to the respective markets, a least-cost location being obtained in respect of each part and the overall least-cost situation being derived from the combination of both. In the case we are considering, sales of produce and services elsewhere are equivalent to the distribution of goods to the market; the purchase of goods and services from outside is analogous to the assembly of raw materials at the point of production.

The principle can be applied fairly easily to settlements that are part of a hierarchical system, as is normally the case in Europe and as is envisaged in most theoretical studies of settlement organization (e.g. Christaller 1966; Lösch 1954). In a hierarchical system, trade transactions take place in a well-defined manner between settlements of higher and lower order, so that the direction and nature of the trade links can be established with some degree of precision. In other contexts, however, trade takes place on a large scale between settlements of the same order and it may be very difficult to identify the pattern relevant for any one settlement. This is particularly true where markets are organized in circuits of varying periodicity (four days, eight days, etc.). Periodic markets are a feature of both east and west Africa, as well as parts of China and elsewhere (Good 1970; Hay 1977; Hodder and Ukwu 1969; R. H. T. Smith 1971). Note that frequently these periodic markets occupy sites where there is no permanent habitation. Whereas Jackson (1971) found that in southern Ethiopia the greatest *minimum* distance to a market is 5 km, the average distance *actually* travelled in the Iboland area of Eastern Nigeria is 10.5 km and in south-west Uganda about 11 km.

Consideration must also be given to other external links in the form of electricity supplies, water and sewerage facilities, telephone and postal services. Most of what needs to be said on this subject is most conveniently reserved to subsequent chapters: in Chapter 6, the importance of such considerations in laying out new settlements in reclamation areas is treated; while the significance of these technical developments for already established populations is tackled in Chapter 8. One general point may be made at this juncture: in the provision of all these services, considerable economies are obtained when the population is concentrated. The more scattered the populace the more costly is the provision of these amenities. Consequently the more remote spots are the last to receive these modern benefits; and as these external links become more important, the advantages of concentrating a dispersed population are becoming greater than formerly was the case.

There is very little quantitative evidence to show the magnitude of the savings which accrue from bringing together scattered dwellings. In any case, the pricing policies adopted by electricity or water authorities, for example, are often such that the individual consumer does not bear the full cost of provision, which makes the task of analysing the matter even more difficult. However, one example can be given which illustrates the point very aptly (see Table 18). From a study of the cost of collecting milk from farms in England and Wales and taking it to the local depot for bulking for onward consignment, it was found that the collection cost varied very closely with the number of gallons collected per mile travelled by the lorry. Gallons per vehicle mile is a measure of the degree of local concentration or dispersal of milk production for sale, compounded of the number of

farms, the production of milk per farm and the arrangement of the
public highways in relation to the farmsteads. From the one point of
view of off-farm collection costs, a high degree of local concentration
of milk production is evidently highly desirable. In this particular
case, it is the Milk Marketing Board that incurs the additional cost of
collection in areas of sparse milk sales and reaps the benefit of
economies where much is collected locally, as the price received by
the farmer does not reflect at all fully the differences in collection
costs. Thus, if there is any incentive towards the local concentration
of milk production to maximize the number of gallons collected per
vehicle, it is felt more by the Board than by the farmers.

Table 18 *England and Wales, 1956: computed costs of milk collection
for contractors handling over two million gallons of milk annually*

Gallons of milk per vehicle mile	Pence per gallon
5	3.786
10	1.678
20	0.883
40	0.582

Source: Chisholm 1957

   The same principle – that concentration confers economies of provision – applies to other services but quantitative information is
sparse and it should not be inferred that the case of milk collection
is necessarily representative. However, it is interesting to note an
estimate that the cost of providing electricity to rural dwellers is
between two and four times the cost of supplying urban inhabitants
(IBRD 1975), a ratio consistent with the data in Table 18.
   The next chapter takes up and elaborates at the small scale the
theme which has been developed in this chapter, and the subsequent
one turns attention to the larger scale of phenomena.

6 The farmstead and the village

Some of the further applications of the principles of location as they operate at the small scale of the individual farmstead or village are now examined. To begin with it is useful to recapitulate in summary form some of the findings discussed in Chapter 3. Table 19 has been prepared on the basis of an estimate of the extent to which the net return per hectare declines with distance, an estimate which is intermediate between the precipitate diminution found to prevail in Finland and Guyana, and the lesser rate of decline indicated for the Netherlands and Pakistan. It has been assumed that all the rural populace lives in nucleated villages of no spatial extent which are distributed regularly, each surrounded by its own territory in the form of a regular hexagon. Since each settlement does in fact have a finite area, the average distance from the farmsteads to the attached land may be slightly less than from the centre of the village, while a further factor contributing to an overstatement of the loss associated with distance is the omission of any consideration of dispersed settlement around the villages. This bias is compensated for by the fact that the territory associated with a village is usually very variable in shape, with the consequence that, for a given average distance between settlements or given area of territory, the average distance to the land is greater than for a regular hexagon.*

* Since the rate of loss incurred becomes less as distance increases it is not sufficient to compute the average distance for a hexagon of a given size and then assign a value for the loss on the basis of this average distance. The hexagons have been built up by adding successive belts one-quarter of a kilometre broad. It was assumed that all the land in each belt did in fact lie at the average distance for that belt. For each belt, a figure could then be assigned for the loss of net product, and in this manner a weighted average loss was obtained for hexagons of the desired size. A selection of the figures which were used for this calculation is shown at the foot of the facing page:

The figures in Table 19 should be taken as representing only a rough order of magnitude. In the construction of this table, the distance between settlements was taken as the datum from which to calculate distances to the land. For practical purposes in relation to

Table 19 *Estimated effect of distance between settlements upon the average net product per hectare*

Distance between settlements (km)	Average distance to cultivated land (km)	Average net product per hectare (zero distance to land equals 100)
0.5	0.18	94
1.0	0.35	90
1.5	0.53	85
2.0	0.70	80
3.0	1.10	72
4.0	1.40	66
6.0	2.11	55
8.0	2.81	47

particular cases, it would be more satisfactory to start from figures for the actual distances separating fields and dwellings. However, such data are not readily available in tabulated form, though the raw information for many countries exists in the cadastral and/or tax records. Given the requisite figures, a very fruitful method of classifying settlement patterns could be based upon the distance between farmstead and field; this would provide material invaluable for planning and development, and significant in describing the relationship between man and his physical environment, probably more useful than is vouchsafed by the currently popular methods of measuring the degree of dispersal and nucleation.

Distance (km)	Net product as per cent
0–0.1	100
0.5	86
1.0	73
1.5	63
2.0	54
3.0	42
4.0	35

Villages and their territories

The settlements of England provide some interesting information
which can be used as a foundation on which to build. Over most of
England, dispersed farmsteads were not generally a part of the early
settlement pattern, though they have subsequently appeared on the
scene. A first, and rather crude, measure of the maximum distance
from settlements to the outer limits of their exploited territories is
given by the evidence summarized by Beresford and St Joseph (1958).
The *minimum* distance between present-day villages averages about
1.6 kilometres for England, which implies that the *minimum*
distance to the territorial limits – the parish boundary – is about 0.8
kilometre.

There are many problems involved in this kind of measurement,
if only that numerous villages which once existed have since been
abandoned. However, given that by the early fourteenth century the
cultivated area had generally expanded to include the whole of a
village's territory, i.e. the parish, and that the parish pattern has been
fairly stable since then, the matter can be pursued in the following
manner. The county of Lincoln, prior to the reorganization of local
government in 1974, was selected as representing the range of shapes
and sizes of parishes found in England; there are also major regional
variations within the county. Taking each parish and its named
village, the median distance to the *furthest* point on the parish boundary is 3.2 kilometres, or four times the *minimum* already quoted.
The regional variations within the county are considerable, as is
shown by Table 20. Boston, Elloe and Spalding Rural Districts
contain areas of reclamation in the Fens, where the progressive in-
take of marshland enabled villages to extend their territory in much
the same way as certain Dutch farms and certain holdings in lower
Canada became very elongated. In these three Rural Districts, the
maximum distance is overstated because in many parishes there is a
second village; the same is true, but in lesser measure, of the other
areas. South Kesteven also contains many long and thin parishes;
in this case they lie transverse to the Jurassic escarpment, thereby
containing a selection of all the soil types locally available, as along
the north edge of the Berkshire Downs. By contrast, where the
physical conditions are more nearly uniform and settlement has been
long-established, the parishes are much more compact, as in Louth,
which contains numerous Wolden villages.

Table 20 *Lincolnshire: median maximum distance from named village to parish boundary* (*km*)

Rural District	Distance
Spilsby	2.3
Grimsby	2.6
Horncastle	2.6
Louth	2.6
Welton	3.0
Caistor	3.2
West Kesteven	3.5
Glandforde Brigg	3.5
East Kesteven	4.0
Isle of Axholme	4.2
South Kesteven	4.2
Boston	5.8
Elloe	7.1
Spalding	8.2
all Lincolnshire	3.2

No very certain conclusions can be drawn from the above evidence, though it is consistent with the following proposition. In the process of crystallization into village units, the pattern which evolved and has survived is one that generally ensures a village having all its territory within a compass of 4.0 kilometres; in Lincolnshire, nearly 70 per cent of the parishes are so constituted. In the majority of cases, all the arable land would be considerably nearer and only the commons and grazing would be at the further limits. Distances of this order are consonant with the evidence which has been presented earlier concerning the magnitude of economic loss associated with the cultivation of distant land, despite the very marked disparity in the levels of technical achievement between our forebears and ourselves. In the present context, the vital technical matter is the means of locomotion and the modern data mostly refer to conditions in which mechanical means of transport on the farm were not much used, so that then as now men walked with their draught animals. But even though distances were kept to reasonable proportions, the costs that they imposed were appreciable, sufficient to cause our forebears to reduce their travel time by establishing satellite settlements.

Satellite settlements

The most rudimentary manifestation of the principle is the platform which some peoples, notably shifting cultivators, erect in the midst of the growing crops to ward off the depredations of birds and animals.

The Bembas of Rhodesia keep them [the ruminants] off by putting up palings. The flights of birds which dart down on the ears of corn are driven off by shouts or volleys of stones. A network of strings is set up over the crop to enable a watchman perched on a platform to sound clappers to frighten away the birds. Certain ingenious Mois have even invented water-driven devices for making protective noises. The cultivators must often leave their villages and temporarily live near the plantation so as to keep a more effective watch. . . . Patches of cassava have the advantage of not needing such close supervision, since animals do not eat the leaves or roots of this plant. [Richards 1958, 307]

Cassava's immunity makes it advantageous to grow the crops which are susceptible – e.g. millets and yams – near at hand, the cassava being placed further away where supervision is more difficult. The construction of temporary platforms becomes necessary when the relevant crops are out of view and/or earshot of the main abode, which commonly means no more than two or three hundred metres. On the other hand, fields of millet may be grown as much as 13 kilometres away, when it becomes necessary to build grass huts to accommodate the family, or a group of related families, during the crop season.

From the numerous published studies of shifting cultivation, it seems quite clear that the principle described by Richards for the Bembas in Rhodesia has a universal application (Öhrling 1977; Pelzer 1945; Spencer 1966; Watters 1971). But satellite settlements are found also among agriculturalists whose main abode is fixed in a permanent place. Such satellite settlements are occupied either seasonally, as on the Alpine pastures, or for short periods on a regular basis. Although the majority of these satellite settlements are located quite near the parent village, two extreme cases call for comment. The inhabitants of M'saken in eastern Tunisia, an agro-town of nearly 30 000 souls of whom perhaps 10 000 are engaged in agriculture, rent land for growing wheat at distances which in extreme cases approach 100 kilometres:

Whole expeditions set out three times a year, and the men, with their teams of mules, their small tents, provisions and equipment, spend weeks at a time away from the town. They leave in the autumn to do their ploughing and sowing; then again at the beginning of spring for weeding; and, finally, in the summer for the harvest. [Dumont 1957, 178–9]

More surprising still is the willingness of the inhabitants of San Pedro Carcha in Guatemala to grow maize 80 kilometres away, transporting it home on their heads (Gourou 1966, 50).

Under conditions in which the population is increasing, satellite settlements which are occupied seasonally may come to be permanently inhabited and to possess a complete economy of their own, independent of the village from which they sprang. This process has been fairly well established as a fact in England from documentary, place-name and topographical evidence, though Darby (1936, 182) sounded a note of warning in saying that 'we do not know enough about the conditions under which the swarming-off from established villages was begun and conducted, and we cannot speculate with any certainty' (see also Sawyer 1976). What we do know indicates that after the Anglo-Saxon and Scandinavian settlement of this country, a considerable amount of waste land was still unoccupied and so remained at the time of the Norman conquest. However, before then, and up to the early fourteenth century, clearance was going on apace. This took two forms: the expansion of the cultivated territory around villages and the establishment of new settlements. Often, these were but two aspects of the same process, the relationship being most apparent in Kent. Here, the waste which surrounded each settlement provided elements essential to its economy – pannage for the pigs, timber and fuel, game and wild fruits. To exploit these resources, it was common for clearances to be made, or natural clearings sought out, where temporary huts might be built to shelter the woodcutters and swineherds. As the population increased, the arable area farmed in common had to be expanded at the expense of the hither waste, involving greater trouble in arable cultivation, wood gathering and the grazing of livestock. Thus, it frequently happened that some of the temporarily occupied clearings came to be permanently inhabited, arable cultivation began and an independent hamlet or village grew up. The suffix *-den* denotes a clearing which was probably used for exploiting the waste, and the Domesday Survey records a number of places in Kent with this ending to their names, distinguishing between those used only for grazing swine, those where arable land was cultivated by villeins and bordars, and, in two cases, fully independent villages – Benenden and Newenden. There are other suffixes which indicate the same process, such as -*ley* and -*field*, -*ergh* and -*booth*. The last two relate to Scandinavian colonization, meaning the summer shieling to which the cattle were taken seasonally, comparable to the Alpine summer villages; since their original foundation, they have come to be permanently inhabited.

Another important pattern of colonization – though not common in Kent – was the enclosure of land at the periphery of the village's cultivated territory. Such enclosed land was hedged and fenced and commonly the farmstead of the peasant was located on the holding. In this fashion the village, with its bare open-fields cultivated in common, might come to be surrounded by a halo of countryside privately farmed, presenting a broken-up appearance. Instead of colonization resulting in a repetition of the previous pattern, a new element was introduced into the landscape which, over the centuries, has achieved dominance, the *coup de grâce* being administered by Parliament in the hundred years from the mid eighteenth century (Beresford and St Joseph 1958; Darby 1936; Hoskins 1955; Lennard 1959).

Subsequent to the writings just cited, a great deal more evidence has come to light confirming the reality and generality of the historical processes outlined above (e.g. Baker and Butlin 1973; Duby 1962; Koebner 1966; Lambert 1971; Mayhew 1971). Indeed, in 1972 Ellison and Harriss attempted to generalize the process in model form and apply their generalizations to a number of selected areas, with highly suggestive results. Furthermore, there is contemporary or quasi-contemporary documentation of the same process. One of the features of Hungary's pattern of settlement is the *tanya*. During the period of Turkish rule, the population was gathered into towns and large villages. After liberation, cultivation spread outwards and, to facilitate this, *tanya* were established at distances of 20 to 30 kilometres from the parent settlements. Initially, the *tanya* were occupied seasonally for wheat cultivation. As farming was intensified, and livestock were introduced, occupation became permanent. Notwithstanding the collectivization of agriculture after the Second World War, the *tanya* have survived as independent, isolated settlements, though functionally linked to the nucleated settlements in that as the *tanya* inhabitants age they move to the villages and towns, being replaced by younger people (Enyedi 1976). On the island of New

Britain in the Pacific, south of the main town of Rabaul, population has been rising and more land has been brought into cultivation:

> The accepted solution, if land can be obtained, seems to be a satellite village four miles [6.4 kilometres] from the main one, or just beyond daily commuting range on foot but within visiting range of the social services of the main village. [Salisbury 1970, 97]

Finally, Galloway (1968) records the establishment of new sugar mills in Pernambuco during the nineteenth century as a response to the problems of expanding the area tributary to existing mills; and Mukerji (1976) describes the recent penetration of settlement along the valleys leading into the Siwalik Hills of India.

There is in fact a full spectrum from the temporary abode occupied only seasonally, through permanent dwellings inhabited on a regular seasonal basis and a highly integrated economic and social system in which it would be invidious to describe one settlement as satellite to another. Permanent but intermittently occupied residences are found at distances beyond that which is convenient for the daily return journey, 3–5.5 kilometres in the case of some Indian cultivators (Blaikie 1971) and about 10 kilometres for Guyanese rice farmers (Richardson 1974). The Yoruba people of western Nigeria appear to have developed a highly articulated system in which large numbers of people are regularly moving between cities and villages, and villages and farm dwellings, over quite astonishing distances. A small sample of farmers in Ibadan, a city of over one million inhabitants, recorded only 15 per cent with their farms within 8 kilometres; 14 per cent had their farms 160 kilometres or more away (Oluwasanmi 1967). The scale of this movement has been documented by Ojo (1973) for one town of approximately 30 000 inhabitants. Data supplied by Ojo show that around Idanre, in association with the fortnightly rhythm of movement, there are 210 'farm villages', housing 'commuting' farmers at distances up to 44 kilometres; although the great majority are located between 4 and 16 kilometres from the main town, no fewer than 53 are at a greater distance. From a survey on the main radial routes from Idanre, conducted over an entire week in 1968, one may estimate that 13000 people travel to/from their farms in a week; of these, only 3670 travelled less than 4.8 kilometres, and 4060 travelled more than 9.6 kilometres. From my own personal observation of Yorubaland in the mid 1960s, and published accounts, it

appears that Idanre is typical of south-west Nigeria for its complex
and far-reaching pattern of urban-farm mobility.

Dispersal of settlements

One of the more dramatic examples of the dispersal of the agricultural
population from nucleated settlements is provided by southern Italy
in the post-war period (King 1973). Immediately after the war,
something like 20 per cent of the agricultural workforce was either
unemployed or underemployed in southern Italy, Sicily and Sardinia.
Industrial and commercial employment on the one hand, and emigra-
tion on the other, were inadequate to cope with this problem.
Therefore, to raise living standards the intensification of agriculture
was essential. With this object in view, the Italian government insti-
tuted in 1950 a series of measures of land reform and agricultural
improvement – irrigation, the introduction of tree crops, cattle rearing, etc.

   Given the highly concentrated pattern of population clusters
(Table 7, page 48), the intensification of agriculture would have
proved prohibitively costly in the absence of some dispersal of dwellings from the agro-towns. The reform agencies set about their task
energetically but by the mid 1960s the programme of works virtually
ceased. However, in the 15 years or so of great activity, 44 000 dispersed farmsteads, nearly 200 residential centres and about 350
service centres were built; it is likely that about 0.2 million people
moved to dispersed settlements, or 2 per cent of the population in
the reform areas (*Annuario dell'Agricoltura Italiana*; King 1973). At
least locally, the result is a remarkable transformation of the rural
landscape; as one travels across the plains of Metaponto or Marem-
ma, one can see for kilometre upon kilometre a guard of honour of
small dwellings, regimented in regular rows, each standing in its own
plot of land. Furthermore, what is grown on the land has changed
dramatically. On the reform lands collectively, the proportion of
uncultivated land dropped sharply (Marciani 1966) and the distribution of the gross saleable product has changed as follows (King 1973):

Year	Arable products (%)	Orchard products (%)	Livestock products (%)
1953	83	6	11
1964	58	18	25

Gross saleable output per hectare rose at 8.5 per cent annually (constant prices) on the lands assigned to the reform programme, compared with an annual growth of only 2.6 per cent in Italy as a whole.

Italy provides but one example of the planned dispersal of residences from large nucleated settlements. An analogous but spontaneous process has been reported from Upper Volta in West Africa (Lahuec 1970). The region is one with a well-established pattern of permanent nucleated settlements dating to the turn of the present century, with associated concentric zoning of crops such as millet, maize and groundnuts. Since about 1930, new dispersed compounds have been established within 1–1.5 kilometres of the parent villages, on land that previously was less intensively used. This dispersal may be ascribed to several factors, including the problem of maintaining soil fertility:

The dispersal of settlements has been beneficial in the sense that it has permitted a more rational use of domestic refuse [as manure], giving each head of household the opportunity to cultivate a field of maize around his dwelling. [Lahuec 1970, 158]

Demangeon (1926 and 1947) described a similar phenomenon in Egypt, where the establishment of scattered farmsteads has been made possible and more desirable by a technical change, the substitution of perennial irrigation for the annual inundations of the basin system which rendered most of the territory useless for permanent homes. At the same time, improvements in the legal status of the *fellaheen*, whereby they may own land, with a certain loosening of the communal forms of social and economic organization, have also tended to ease dispersal, which has been quite marked since the mid nineteenth century.

Likewise, in Thailand many small, isolated settlements and individual farmsteads have been established in the last half century. True of the central areas, this development has been especially marked in the delta region near Bangkok, throughout much of which compact villages have ceased to be the distinctive element of the settlement pattern (de Young 1955). And in Mexico, too, the process of dispersal from the villages has begun. Traditionally a country in which the population lives in large communities, some dispersal has been associated with irrigation and other reclamation schemes but in addition villagers are beginning to move out of their settlements and establish their homes on the land they till. This is particularly notable in Mexicali valley, at the head of the Gulf of California (Whetten 1948). Even in Fiji, where the average village has fewer than 100 inhabitants, a move towards dispersal has become evident since about 1960 (Frazer 1973).

Yet another reason for the dispersal of farmsteads resides in the programmes of consolidation undertaken by most west European countries since the last war. Consolidation means the re-allocation of holdings which are fragmented, the creation of farms which comprise only one or a very few parcels in place of the multitude of patches formerly in the possession of each peasant. At the same time, roads are re-aligned, drainage improved, water supplies made available, better systems of farming introduced and perhaps some farmsteads re-located. The magnitude of the task that has been undertaken by governments and private organizations in Europe is indicated by the data in Table 21.

Table 21 *Europe: land consolidation*

Country	Total agricultural area 1971 (million hectares)	Area consolidated (million hectares)	Area still to be consolidated 1971 (million hectares)	Average annual consolidation (hectares)	Average cost per hectare (dollars)
Austria	1.54	0.472 (1971)	0.850	25 000 (1967–70)	250
France	30.83	6.90 (1971)	15.000	470 000 (1966–69)	170
West Germany	12.85	5.029 (1971)	10.100	286 000 (1967–72)	700
Netherlands	2.25	0.435 (1972)	1.140	50 000 (1967–69)	1400
Spain	20.00	4.000 (1973)	1.600	366 000 (1967–72)	50
Switzerland	1.23	0.190 (1971)	0.360	5100 (1968–70)	800

Source: FAO 1976. Cf. Jacoby 1959
Note that the data are not strictly comparable between nations

Wherever possible, the new holding is laid out to include the owner's existing residence; if this policy be pushed to its logical conclusion, the farms would tend to be triangular in shape, the apexes being in the village and containing the farmstead; the farms would form a star centred on the village (Thorpe 1951). Experience with this type of consolidation in Denmark and elsewhere has shown that it produces farms which are awkward to operate. It may well be that a considerable proportion of the farms could not be laid out so as to include the farmstead in its old location – especially where the villages are large. In the case of the land reform in Russia after the revolution of 1905–6, about nine out of ten new holdings did not include the farmstead of the operator (Gubsky 1921). Therefore, the common current policy is to move some of the farmsteads from the village on to their holdings, so that the pattern of settlement produced is one of a central village from which some farms are operated, surrounded by a number of isolated farmsteads. Such relocation, which is especially frequent in West Germany and Switzerland, occurs generally when there is land situated 3 or more kilometres from the village, but also when the distance to the further lands is less (Jacoby 1959). Between 1956 and 1973, 23 112 farmsteads were relocated in West Germany with government aid, as part of the consolidation programme (FAO 1976). However, as Mayhew (1971) notes, re-location of farmsteads is expensive and an alternative is to improve the roads and hence accessibility. Therefore, the more recent practice in Germany is to minimize re-location and invest in road improvements.

Outside Europe, only a very few countries have embarked on major programmes of land consolidation, notably Chile, Egypt, Japan, Korea, Pakistan and Taiwan, and some states in India. Elsewhere in the world, the problem remains to be tackled.

These measures for the reconstruction of the countryside, to create a more dispersed form of settlement pattern, are conscious efforts to achieve a situation which has existed for many years in Norway, Sweden, the United Kingdom and Denmark. In Denmark, the movement to achieve this objective gathered real momentum with the legislation of 1781 to consolidate land and of 1788 to emancipate the peasantry from its feudal bond to the soil. One result of the reforming zeal was the establishment of unitary holdings in place of the openfields worked in common and the consequent appearance of isolated farmsteads set on their own land. Under the 1781 Act, provision was made for public money to be available for the construction of these new farmsteads in cases where the most distant land of a new farm was more than 0.9 kilometre from the old dwelling (Kampp 1975). As early as 1807, the process of transformation had been completed in many districts, while by 1835 practically the whole agricultural area had experienced this revolution (Skovgard 1953; Skrubbeltrang 1953). The consolidation process had begun earlier in Finland, with legislation enacted in 1757; with that and subsequent 'partitions', it was not uncommon for the existing timber buildings to be physically moved to new locations, instead of new ones being built (Mead 1953). Perhaps the earliest recorded attempts in Europe to encourage consolidation can be traced to some Italian cities, which in the twelfth and thirteenth centuries passed laws for this purpose, mainly in the north and especially the Lombardy plain (Jones 1966).

In the English-speaking world, the most famous programme of consolidation is undoubtedly the parliamentary enclosure which occurred in England between about 1750 and 1850, comparable for its success with the Danish and Scandinavian enterprises (Dovring 1965b): it continued and completed a process that had been going on for centuries. By the use of parliamentary powers, coercion replaced consent and the rate of change was much accelerated. Under the traditional open-field system of cultivation in common, each peasant was allotted a certain number of strips, the locations of which were scattered. Quite apart from tenurial relations with regard to the lord of the manor and the necessity for communal regulation and co-operation for certain tasks, the scattering of the strips provided a cogent reason for living together in nucleated villages because this minimized the total distance from the dwellings to the parcels. Enclosure swept away the old system. In its stead, individual ownership of all land became normal, the strips were consolidated into unitary holdings and roads and ditches were re-aligned. Wherever possible, these new farms were laid out to include the pre-existing dwelling of the owner but many farms were inevitably situated at a considerable remove and were therefore separated from the farmstead.

In such cases it was to the obvious advantage of the farmer to build himself a new farmstead in the middle of his lands.

This, indeed, is what happened in due course, but the old village was far from disintegrated by such new building unless it was already very small and decaying. Often many years elapsed before the village farmers built their new houses, however inconvenient it may have been to live in the centre of the parish and to farm on the boundaries. . . .

Yet the total number of farmsteads built out in the fields between the villages is very small. One would guess not more than half a dozen in the average parish, often fewer than thát. . . .

Nevertheless a new element had been introduced into the landscape in this part of England – the isolated farmstead. Nearly all the farm-houses we see between the compact villages of the country between the Yorkshire and the Dorset coasts date from the century 1750–1850. The few that are older may well be either the result of Tudor or Stuart enclosure, or examples of monastic granges. . . . But probably four out of five of these farmsteads in the fields are the consequence of parliamentary enclosure. [Hoskins 1955, 157 and 159]

Williams (1972) noted that with the enclosure of waste land on Mendip for nearly forty years the new farms were operated from the old farmsteads. When a new set of buildings was eventually constructed, the cost amounted to roughly one-fifth to one-quarter of the total cost of establishing the new farm.

Farm consolidation and the associated dispersal of farm dwellings will serve to increase the net agricultural output and/or reduce the total labour requirements. Because changes in farming practice and net output result from numerous separate modifications to the farming system – enlargement of fields, improvement of access, mechanization, etc. – it is impossible accurately to identify the contribution made by the reduction in distance between dwelling and field. Jacoby (1959) states that the gross yield of a holding may rise between 20 and 70 per cent as a result of consolidation. Experience in Austria indicates that on average the labour force is actually reduced by 14 per cent (Jacoby 1959); other studies indicate that for a given gross income, labour requirements are reduced by between 5 and 50 per cent (Schuler 1957). Taking two model settlement patterns for irrigated agriculture in southern Ceylon, Weitz *et al.* (1971) arrived at the following conclusions. Where the dispersed dwelling is situated next to the field crops, the padi fields might be up to 0.8 kilometre away from the home village, and the local service centres not more than 3.2 kilometres from the remotest farmstead; under these circumstances, approximately 137 kilometres would be walked each year between home and farmland. If, on the other hand, all the population lived in nucleated settlements, the equivalent distance would be 676 kilometres. The annual saving in time would represent somewhat less than 5 per cent of total working time, but perhaps 10 or 15 per cent of agricultural time.

Experience in India is instructive. Agarwal (1971) selected two groups of villages, one in which consolidation had occurred and another control group in which it had not. In fact, the consolidation was only partial, as the following figures for the number of plots per operational holding (as distinct from ownership holding) show:

	Project villages	Control villages
Before consolidation	5.4	6.1
After consolidation	3.3	6.1

No re-location of dwellings took place. In the control villages, total labour input, including travel time, amounted to 104 man-days per hectare, compared with 100 in the villages where consolidation had occurred. The saving therefore amounted to 4 per cent of the agricultural labour input. But this does not take account of the extra time spent actually working on the land. Taking the gross value of outputs and gross value of inputs, Agarwal found that *net* output was increased by a factor of between 5 and 6.

An alternative approach to the problem starts with the data in Table 19 (page 107). If we assume that the *average* distance between the farmsteads and fields (not the distance between settlements) is reduced by one half-kilometre, the gross yield of a given area will increase by between 6 and 7 per cent. A reduction in distance of this magnitude is greater than the 10 per cent reduction estimated to have been achieved in Dutch reorganization schemes (Bijkerk 1973), but is consistent with Finnish experience. In the latter country, modern reorganization programmes reduced the national average distance to plots by between 0.1 and 0.2 kilometre (Pihkala and Suomela 1952), implying a substantially greater reduction for the properties actually affected. A modest diminution in average distance will clearly make an appreciable direct contribution to increasing both gross and net output, as well as facilitating innumerable beneficial side effects.

The gains may not be equally distributed and some sections of the rural populace may be worse off, as proved to be the case in Kenya:

The criticism that consolidation initially creates unemployment and landlessness is a valid one. In the Central Province the landowner possessing many fragments was frequently unable to cultivate all of them and so allowed tenants (*ahoi*) to cultivate the least desirable and more remote of these fragments ... [consolidation creates unemployment] until such time as the labour demands of the developing holdings outstrip the capacity of the farmer and his family, at which time some of the landless will be absorbed as labour. [Republic of Kenya 1966, 19]

To meet this kind of problem, the Dutch are implementing a careful programme in an attempt to improve and rationalize the agrarian structure. Measures of consolidation are in hand which tend to reduce the need for labour and, to absorb the surplus, active steps are being taken to provide new industrial employment within the areas affected, whereby a change of work does not necessarily require a change of habitation. As a parallel measure, farms are reserved in the newly reclaimed polders to accommodate farmers displaced by the consolidation schemes.

Problems of dispersal

Dispersal of the rural population does raise some awkward problems under two headings: (1) the costs of providing roads and public utilities such as electricity and water, which are greater than where everyone lives in compact settlements; (2) the loneliness which often characterizes life on isolated farms, which may be specially burdensome for those accustomed to the society of village life. Therefore, in practice it is now common for a number of compromise solutions to be attempted and a discussion of these occupies the next few paragraphs (Takes 1958 and 1975; van Dusseldorp 1971).

To allow for varying degrees of soil fertility and differences in the sizes, abilities and resources of farm families, it is desirable that farms within an area should be of various sizes. In laying out an entirely new area, such as a Dutch polder, the most satisfactory arrangement of the territory, viewed solely from the farm management point of view, would be square holdings, with the farmstead located centrally. The square is the most economical shape – in the sense of minimizing the average distance from the centre to the land – that permits the whole territory to be laid out in units of varying area and simultaneously is convenient for arable farm operations. Depending on the nature of the cultivation techniques and the total farm area, an oblong may be a better shape for facilitating farming. The two primary shapes, therefore, are the square and oblong (Lee and Sallee 1974). With these considerations in mind, Figure 10 illustrates the balancing of factors. The layout in Figure 10*b* requires the same total length of road as in 10*a* but half the track (the spurs to the farmsteads) can be built to specifications lower than is needed for the public highway; similar savings can be obtained for services such as water, electricity and sewerage. Compared with Figure 10*a*, there is also a slightly greater facility for social intercourse. In Figure 10*c*, the route length for all services is halved and opportunities for social interaction are sharply increased; however, as the farmsteads are no longer central in the farm, the expenses of cultivation are somewhat increased. If the square is abandoned (Figure 10*d*), even greater economies in laying out the reclamation area can be obtained, the farmsteads can conveniently be located at one corner of the holding to form groups of four, but the farm running expenses again rise. The actual solution adopted is generally based upon Figures 10*c* and 10*d*, and depends upon the estimates of the costs of laying out the area, balancing savings on that score against increases in the expenses of managing the farms. This is a problem that lends itself to formal project evaluation in terms of benefit–cost analysis, something that the Dutch have in fact undertaken in planning the Ijssel Meer polder reclamations.

Modern Dutch planning adopts the principle illustrated in Figure 10*d*. However, whereas the standard farm used to be 24 hectares, measuring 300 metres by 800, the more recent reclamations provide both for a variety of farm sizes and a larger norm; Southern Flevoland is the newest polder, and farms of 60 hectares (500×1200 metres) are standard (Constandse 1974). Some of the reclamations carried out in Italy under Mussolini were laid out in a similar fashion, whereas some more recent projects in that country have adopted the model in Figure 10*c*.

Where, as in the Dutch polders, the territory is laid out with reference to villages which provide social and shopping facilities and may also act as a collecting point for farm produce and source of farm supplies, it is desirable that so far as possible the smaller farms should be located near the village and the larger further away. In this manner, for a given structure of farm sizes, the total costs of movement between the farms and the village will be minimized, taking the whole territory. This particular point was influential in the enclosure of Ireland's County Tipperary in the following modified manner. With enclosure, the whole lowland was reorganized into square fields and consolidated holdings. The larger farms had cen-

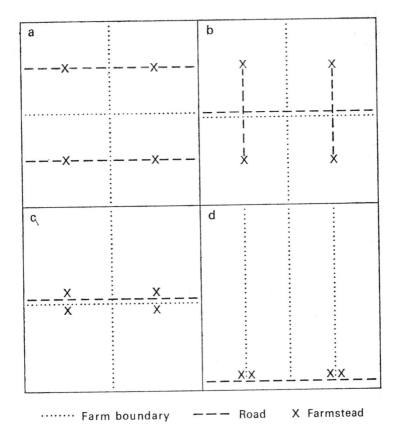

.... Farm boundary   — — — Road   X Farmstead

Figure 10   *Rural road patterns*

trally located farmsteads, while the medium to small farms – between 20 and 80 hectares – were laid out with the dwellings situated along the roads (Leister 1976).

Another form of compromise adopted by the Dutch in recent years is to provide dwellings for wage labourers in the villages rather than on the holdings. Formerly, all the wage hands would live on or adjacent to the farm, but in the newer reclamation schemes provision is there made only for key workers such as the stockmen, who must be available at any time. The other workers are able to live in the village and therefore have readier access to the amenities of social living;

perhaps equally important, their dwellings are not owned by their employer, which makes it possible for them to change jobs without forfeiting the roof over their head. For such workers, a village location provides a greater choice of readily accessible employers than would be the case with scattered residences (Constandse 1957). This compromise is only possible where there is wage labour, and in Spain and Italy another solution has been essayed to meet the needs of a peasant society in which very little labour is hired. In both countries, experiments are being conducted with small residential villages where the farming fraternity live, their farms surrounding the community at no very great distance. Precisely the same system has developed in Sabah, Malaysia, in order to reduce infrastructure costs, which were high in the early projects of dispersed farmsteads (Sutton 1977).

Quite apart from the problem of infrastructure costs, account must be taken of the willingness or otherwise of settlers to live in dispersed, and therefore lonely, dwellings. Long-enduring cultural conditions have an important bearing in this respect. As long ago as 1945, Pelzer noted that settlement schemes organized under American rule in the Philippines in the period 1912–35 had not been satisfactory, precisely because the local tradition of village life was inconsistent with American concepts of land division. Uganda provides another example, with between one-quarter and one-third of plots on group farm schemes unoccupied, largely on account of loneliness (Charsley 1968). Thus, the plea by Preston (1974) for more research on the layout of settlement schemes, made with respect to Latin America and the widely varying social conditions in that continent, has a general application.

Concentration of settlements

So far, we have discussed various aspects of the dispersal of population from existing nucleated settlements but dispersal is not the universal trend. Where constraints of one kind or another have been removed, the spontaneous tendency has generally been for many farmsteads to be shifted from the nucleated settlements; where, locally, the constraints have become more severe, the reverse process has happened in the past and is even today occurring. A particular consideration is that of security and military requirements, especially under conditions of guerrilla warfare. Approximately 0.6 million people had been forcibly grouped into villages in Malaya by 1954, some villages containing over 5000 inhabitants (Ooi 1963; Sandhu 1964); the Kenyan Mau Mau emergency saw the 'villagization' of over 1.0 million inhabitants (Apthorpe and MacArthur 1968). Algeria has experienced a similar programme which affected 2.2 million people, or 24 per cent of the Muslim population (Lesne 1962). Prior to granting independence to Mozambique, the Portuguese attempted to check the Frelimo guerrillas by a resettlement programme that uprooted 1.0 million Africans (*The Times* 12 February 1974); India did the same to 0.2 million Mizos, or two-thirds of the Mizo ethnic group (*The Times* 28 May 1969); and Rhodesia has followed suit with a programme involving 47 000 (*The Times* 29 June 1974). Finally, a significant element of Israel's agricultural workforce lives in urban areas and commutes to the fields as a response to guerrilla incursions by Palestinian forces (Berler 1970).

Given the military constraints affecting the choice of sites, and the military convenience of having a few large nucleations, it is to be expected that with the ending of emergency conditions people would move out of the villages to be nearer their land. This has certainly happened in Malaya where the villagization programme resulted in a sharp drop in agricultural output; of the 438 new villages which existed in 1954, 38 are known to have been empty six years later. Similarly, between 1957 and the mid 1960s, most of the new Kikuyu villages had been abandoned (Sorrenson 1967). On the other hand, it appears that the Algerian villages have survived better (de Planhol 1961). Also the villages created in the Tonga Islands at the end of the eighteenth century to provide security for the inhabitants during the internecine strife which lasted into the first half of the nineteenth century have survived. After fifty years of enforced village life, peace was restored and a new allocation of lands became possible:

and although this meant travelling some distance from the house to grow food, the advantages of village life were sufficiently great to cause the village pattern to be retained . . . and this in spite of the fact that, with the years, land allocation, which may place a farm several miles from the village, has increased the inconvenience of such a settlement pattern. [Kennedy 1958, 164–5]

Whether in fact forcibly created villages survive the ending of hostilities seems to depend on a complex interplay of the nature of the sites chosen, the size of the villages, the duration of the emergency and the extent to which facilities (clinics, schools, etc.) are provided.

If not military, then ideological considerations may lead to the concentration of the rural population. The Spanish conquest of Mexico and Guatemala was followed by the forcible resettlement of the Indian population. This sixteenth-century process was initially undertaken in the name of religion and was in the hands of missionaries; however, the civil authorities took over between 1598 and 1625. Although attempts were made to choose sites suitable for agriculture, the resettlement of the aborigines in central and southern Mexico 'sometimes had dire consequences. The environs were often unsuitable for Indian agriculture, with the result that food production decreased and famine ensued' (West and Augelli 1966, 272). Nevertheless, by the mid seventeenth century compact agricultural villages had become an integral part of the Mexican landscape and have survived the land reform programmes of the twentieth century. A modern counterpart to the Spanish policies in Middle America is provided by the USSR. From 1959, there was forcible concentration of the rural population into villages of 1000 and more, partly to facilitate the provision of schools and other services, but partly as a means of maintaining political/ideological control of the peasantry, and in the conviction that collective forms of agriculture were both desirable and a suitable means for ensuring the delivery of prescribed quotas. By 1968, some of the ill-effects of this policy had become apparent and thereafter, although concentration remained the aim, satellite and dormitory villages were tolerated so that agriculture could be conducted more efficiently. The larger villages created in this programme of concentration are losing population (Pallot 1977; see also Dovring 1965*b*).

Finally, we may note the programme initiated in Tanzania in 1962, to re-group the rural population into villages of about 250 inhabitants. The purpose was to make the provision of schools, water supplies, village industries, etc., easier, as well as to help with the improvement of agriculture. It appears that relatively little progress had been made until the 1970s, when great strides were made (Newiger 1968; Hirst 1978).

Summary of evidence

A point which emerges from the preceding discussion and the material of Chapter 3 is the frequency with which the same orders of magnitude keep on recurring among people of widely different technical achievements and inhabiting areas with markedly different physical characteristics. Any distance up to about a kilometre from the dwelling is of such little moment for any but specialized systems of irrigation and garden farming that little adjustment is called for in either the pattern of settlement or of land use. Beyond about 1 kilometre, the costs of movement become sufficiently great to warrant some kind of response; at a distance of 3–4 kilometres the costs of cultivation necessitate a *radical* modification of the system of cultivation or settlement – for example by the establishment of subsidiary settlements – though adjustments are apparent before this point is reached. If the distances involved are actually greater than this, then it is necessary to look for some very powerful constraining reason which prevents the establishment of farmsteads nearer the land. Over much of the world, the present spontaneous tendency is to modify the patterns of rural settlement and land holding in such a manner that the distance separating the farmstead from the lands cultivated is reduced to something in the order of 1 or 2 kilometres, if the farmstead is not actually on the farm. Apart from the cases of forcible concentration, there is also some tendency for wage labourers and even owner-occupiers to move to villages near their farms, but this occurs generally only in the more advanced nations (see Chapter 8). The tendency to dispersal is not apparent in Australia, Canada, the United States and elsewhere, where the farmsteads have for long been located on unitary holdings.

Land taxation

An interesting practical application of location principles is found in the taxation of agricultural land. In those countries where it operates, the tax is levied on the assessed value of the property, which may be its market value were it sold, or the level of net income derived from its operation. In some countries, an attempt is made to assess each individual plot; this necessarily means taking account of the location of each parcel with respect to the farmstead, to arrive at the true worth – the value of the produce less the costs of cultivation. Such practices are followed in several European countries (van Aartsen 1944), in the West Indies (Paget 1961), and in Burma and parts of India, notably Madras and Bombay (Wald 1959). It appears that the practice used to be quite widespread in India under British rule, given the need to raise revenue by land taxes; in the absence of market data on land values, an assessment system had to be developed by which to estimate land values (Joshi *et al.* 1968; Neale 1962). Such a system came into general use in Uttar Pradesh in 1875, distinguishing three distance zones around each village, but subsequently fell into disuse as better information became available for individual proprietors. By contrast, in the Punjab other considerations appear to have been more important (Douie 1915).

Work study

This chapter is aptly concluded with a few sentences on another practical micro-application of location principles. Work study, or time-and-motion study, is a technique which has been developed primarily by engineers, especially in connection with manufacturing industry, but the methods have spread to agriculture, administration and commerce. The basic principle is simple: all production, assembly and distribution within a firm (factory, farm or office) requires the movement of goods and persons from point to point, or the repetition of the same sequence of operations by individual persons. Work study seeks to record and measure these movements and then to devise alternative arrangements which will reduce the total amount of movement required to achieve given objectives to the minimum that is possible. This is essentially an exercise in the relative positions of objects and the paths of movement which are traced between them in an attempt to achieve a least-cost location pattern (if the amount of production is to be constant) or a maximum profit one (if the output of the existing labour force is to be increased to the maximum).

The point is well illustrated by a case quoted by Piel-Desruisseaux (n.d.) in which the reorganization of a farm's dairy buildings resulted in a saving of about 63 per cent in the *kilogram-metres* required for their operation (Table 22). Sturrock (1958) found that for tending 50 bullocks the number of man-hours required per week varied from 12 to 60 in accordance with the layout adopted.

To date, location principles have been mainly applied to particular jobs, such as the tending of cattle or the sorting of fruit. But in principle, there is no reason why work study should not encompass the spatial arrangement of the whole farm, thereby extending to the whole the logic of what is meet for the part. Indeed, although the

Table 22 *Reorganization of farm buildings* (*thousand kilogram-metres of work per day*)

Commodity	Before	After
cream	150	550
grain	550	—
clover, straw, silage	3720	2290
whole milk	3485	255
separated milk	3165	975
total	11 070	4070

Source: Piel-Desruisseaux, n.d., vi–5

works published in English are silent on this point, Piel-Desruisseaux is quite explicit, pointing out that the spatial arrangement of buildings, means of access and types of enterprise are closely interrelated. He advocates the advantages of having near the farm those enterprises which require much transport and further away those which require less, taking account of all operations.

Some farm advisory workers in the United Kingdom are in fact applying this principle. Imperial Chemical Industries Ltd provides an advisory service for farmers which has the object of raising the net income of the farms which participate. One of the means to this end is intensification of the use of the land to increase the per hectare yields, with carefully controlled rotations, grazing and management. As it is not possible to effect this improvement suddenly over the whole farm, a beginning is usually made with one or two fields; the success achieved on these then provides the lessons which may be applied elsewhere on the holding. The field chosen for the initial development is always near the farmstead; as additional fields are brought into the intensive system, they form a ring round the dwelling. In time, this ring is expanded outwards to the periphery of the farm, and if it is small enough the whole area will be lifted to a higher level of productivity. Where the farm is large, it may be necessary to leave a peripheral belt which will continue to be farmed at a markedly lower level of intensity, on account of the costs of operation being too high to warrant the more intensive cultivation.

7   The region and the world: 2

This chapter falls into two parts of unequal length. The first and longer section is concerned with the relatively simple but neglected problem of the location of lines of communication with respect to rural and urban needs or potential needs. The second part is designed to round off the picture by showing that the explanation for differing densities of rural population in the various parts of the world requires one step of argument which places the discussion into the locational framework that is being developed in this book.

Location of a transport route

We have seen that in considering the destination of produce and the source of inputs, remembering the various stages of marketing, it is desirable to include not only inhabited centres, which may be treated as points, but also traffic arteries. These may be regarded as continuous lines, even though access to them is limited to relatively few specified places. An important problem arises each time there is a proposal to build a new route, be it of whatever kind, i.e. where shall it be located? Many consequences turn upon the answer, among them the profitability of the transport enterprise, the effectiveness of the transport service to be provided, changes in land use and production and the development of urban centres. In a limited number of cases, there is no effective choice between routes because the costs incurred in using any but the 'obvious' one would be too great. To connect New York by canal with the Great Lakes by any means other than the Hudson–Mohawk alignment would have involved enormous additional expenses which could easily be recognized and which would have yielded no return. Or if a road is to be built between Fort William and Inverness, how otherwise could it be aligned than along the Great Glen? But in the generality of cases, there is a greater choice and consequently a nice problem of location is presented.

Initially, let us imagine the construction of a new railway line, whether by a private company or public corporation. The basic aim will be to situate the railway where the amount of actual or potential traffic which may be tapped per route kilometre is at a maximum. This is subject to the reservation that, in choosing a route which maximizes the traffic per unit distance of track, the construction and running costs are not raised unduly; if they are, then a compromise solution must be sought. For example, the shorter of alternative alignments may tap a greater amount of traffic per kilometre of way, but involve steep gradients and curves of small radius which raise construction costs and running expenses to such a level that the longer route proves to be more advantageous.

A simple example may be taken to illustrate the matter. Suppose that it is intended to build a railway through a strip of territory some 5 kilometres broad, comprising a level plain in which the land is disposed in five bands running parallel with the general direction of the railway. The land outside this swathe of 5 kilometres is quite uncultivated; within it, the five bands are disposed as in Figure 11: band A represents the best quality of soil for farming, C and C_1 the poorest, while B and B_1 are intermediate in fertility. The consequence of these differing degrees of fertility is that the total produce of a square kilometre plus the requisite inputs of fertilizer, etc., amounts to 1000 tonnes annually for the best land, 750 and 500 respectively for the intermediate and worst soil. We will further suppose that access to the railway is possible at all points. Then, since we may assume that the costs of constructing and running the railway are not affected by the alignment which is chosen within the belt of territory, the problem of location resolves itself into that which will minimize the cost of getting goods to and from the line, which is to minimize the tonne-kilometres required.

Let the first choice of alignment be XX, and consider then a segment of territory *defg* measuring 5 kilometres by 1. If the average distance from the railway to each of the three categories of land is multiplied by the tonnage of goods to be taken to and from the line, it will be found that the tonne-kilometres required for access to the railway amount to 3750 each year. Should the route YY be chosen, the figure would be 3960, while ZZ would entail a total of 4687 tonne-kilometres; any more eccentric position would involve even greater costs of access to the route. In this hypothetical case, the optimum

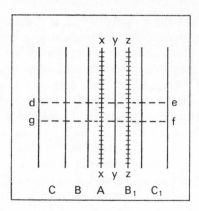

Figure 11 *Location of a single route*

location is XX and any deviation from XX results in additional and unnecessary expenses.

It may well be that all of these expenses of movement to and from the railway are borne by persons other than the railway company. If this were so, then on the assumptions made so far the investor would be indifferent as to the route chosen, the reason being that we have assumed a given volume of traffic per square kilometre. Such an assumption is clearly contrary to evidence which has already been cited in this book, and is disproved by the extensive literature on the modelling of freight flows, in which gravity-model formulations are common (e.g. Chisholm and O'Sullivan 1973). Thus, in the hypothetical example cited above, the notional tonnes per hectare apply only if the zone in question is immediately adjacent to the railway. Consequently, for each possible alignment, a downward adjustment of the freight volume must be made for the relevant soil categories to allow for their distances from the railway. With such adjustment, the penalty attached to locating other than at XX arises in the form of reduced levels of traffic on the railway.

For the purpose of exposition, a simple case has been selected but the principle is applicable generally. Wherever there is territory which varies in its capacity to generate traffic, it will normally be advantageous to locate a new route as close as possible to those areas which actually do, or potentially will, give rise to the most business. Exactly the same is true of improvements to existing facilities: where there is a choice of projects, it is a better economic proposition to renovate or replace where existing traffic demand is greatest, rather than in the less congested areas (see page 136).

In practice, although the greater part of a communications system usually lies in rural areas, the basic layout of the network is generally more influenced by urban and industrial needs than by rural and agricultural requirements. Therefore, it is hardly relevant to discuss the problem of where to locate a new route other than in the context of the economy as a whole, though the principles which are involved are identical to those outlined above. The matter was treated at considerable length by Wellington (1898), an engineer who was responsible for planning the location of the Mexican railways. Two of his observations are specially relevant. He estimated that the adverse effect upon gross revenue of placing a station away from the centre of a town amounted to a reduction of 10 per cent for each 1.6 kilometres in the case of a small country town without a competitive alternative and 25 per cent for large industrial cities possessing competing railway facilities. This is an effect analogous to the smaller amount of traffic which will be generated by a plot of agricultural land the further removed it is from the railway. Second, he considered that if a line were going to be built between two points, and if all intermediate points were of equal traffic-generating capacity and were equally spaced, then the amount of traffic on the line would vary as the square of the number of the points served. This then justifies quite considerable detours to link up such sources of traffic.

Wellington was writing at a time when modern road transport had yet to be developed and therefore when movement tributary to a railway was more difficult than it now is; therefore, his empirical values are probably no longer valid for new construction, but they were eminently important when much of the present-day network of the world was being built.

The fundamental proposition which has been made above, that if conditions of the physical environment and economic development are known and the construction of a new transport artery or system is contemplated, then the layout of communications is the variable factor, finds its application in the study of Bourrières (1950). From the production data available, he calculated the value of output per square kilometre in the different parts of the Ivory Coast and found that it was highest in the southern forest zone, lowest in the north and intermediate in the savanna areas. On this basis, his recommendations envisaged the densest network of road and rail routes in the forest regions, the sparsest network in the further interior. These recommendations accorded with the then existing relative densities of the communication systems in the different parts of the country. Furthermore, in the neighbouring state of Ghana, Gould (1960) traced the evolution of the road network at selected dates over the period 1900 to 1958. After the initial thrust of roads inland from the coast, the densest network quickly built up in the southern part of the country, though with subsidiary centres of high density in the north, reflecting relatively favourable environmental conditions.

This general theme has been examined by Glover and Simon (1975). For 113 nations, excluding island states such as Hong Kong and Malta, the authors obtained the density of the road network in 1968. This was treated as the dependent variable to be explained by two independent variables – namely population density and income per caput. Using an equation in logarithms, the authors obtained a value for R^2 of 0.83, demonstrating a quite exceptional level of correlation. This international cross-section study confirms the validity of the intra-national studies which have been cited (see also Hoyle 1973).

A rather different line of evidence is provided by the nineteenth-century history of railway construction. In Britain, the railways were built by private companies which had obtained parliamentary consent for the particular route; amalgamations also had to be sanctioned by an Act. Thus, fortunes were made and lost in a battle conducted at the political and financial level: political, because votes in Parliament had to be wooed and won; financial, because money had to be enticed into bonds. It was also an economic battle between the railways and the canals and roads, and between competing railway companies. If there were three kinds of move – political, financial and economic – available to the promoters of new lines or of amalgamations, there was only one arena – a chessboard of locations. Recurrent themes therefore emerge.

First, the earliest routes to be built were those where there was an already existing demand for transport facilities, particularly for the movement of coal:

The chief reason why the railways came into existence was because of the need of more adequate facilities for conveyance than the canals could give. The enormous profits which some canals were making were also an inducement for railways to come in and secure a share of these benefits, and the success of existing railroads, giving additional encouragement to the projectors of new lines, had an important effect in initiating these enterprises along routes where they were much needed. [Jackman 1916, 514]

After the opening of the Stockton–Darlington line in 1825, to supply an existing need for mineral transport – a canal had been projected for the same purpose – the next major lines were all built by local interests to break canal monopolies: Liverpool–Manchester, Liverpool–Birmingham, Birmingham–London, London–Bristol. The succeeding projects which actually materialized were to connect existing centres between which much traffic already flowed, for example Newcastle–Carlisle, London–Southampton and Leeds–Hull. An examination of the railway network at 1840 and 1850, as given by Wilfred Smith (1953), shows quite clearly how the first lines linked up centres which generated a lot of traffic.

Second, if occasionally the early lines were built where there was little previous traffic movement, it was because the promoters anticipated a good potential of trade, hopes which were not always realized.

Third, the battles to obtain concessions for routes, to reach working agreements with, and to take over, other companies, were fundamentally struggles to control lucrative traffic. Though political, financial and managerial skills were requisite, these would avail nothing if the company chose a poor route to operate or was subsequently outmanoeuvred in the locational struggle. The two stations possessed by many towns in England, such as Reading, Nottingham and Leicester, is testimony to the attempts made to secure traffic and drive out competitors in an effort to develop and maintain regional monopolies such as that achieved by the North Eastern in the area between Berwick, Hull and the Pennine foothills. Gloucester was one of the early strategic prizes, for when the Great Western linked this city to its line from London, any possible incursion of Midland companies into the south-west was effectively barred and at the same time the Great Western gained access to South Wales, enabling it to project and ultimately complete a line to Fishguard to capture much of the Irish trade.

Exactly the same kind of drama has been enacted upon the American stage. In the period after the depression of 1884:

The strife between railroad systems in the West became more virulent and was the force behind an increasing proportion of railroad construction. Within a few years three new routes were completed between Chicago and

Kansas City. One was by the Atchison, Topeka & Santa Fé to strengthen its bargaining power with its eastern connections, another by the Chicago, Milwaukee & St Paul to increase its control of western traffic, and a third by one of the predecessors of the present Minneapolis & St Louis. [Healy 1940, 12]

There can be no doubt that the early history of the railways in the United Kingdom, United States and elsewhere was of competition, with the object of establishing local and regional monopolies, taking place within a matrix of alternative locations, each offering different advantages. Success depended in part upon the skill with which these advantages were evaluated. A full understanding of railway history cannot be obtained unless the events are viewed as an exercise in the practical economics of location, as is amply demonstrated by Grodinsky (1962) in his study of railway development in the United States. Furthermore, such knowledge facilitates an understanding of the present-day problems of mergers between companies and the reduction in the size of the network that are a feature of many developed states.

Finally, the construction of motorways in post-war Britain provides yet another example. Between the opening of the first major section of the M1 in 1959 and 1977 the main elements of the new network took shape, forming a narrow-waisted H centred on Coventry–Birmingham. The limbs extend to Exeter, London, Carlisle and Leeds, with major road improvements extending further north to Scotland. The figure has been completed by east–west links between Newport and London, and Liverpool and Leeds, and a series of motorways radiating from London. Even a quick look at the map will show that this basic layout links up the major conurbations along routes with a heavy load of traffic. Indeed, the configuration of the network planned by the then Ministry of Transport was explicitly designed to relieve traffic congestion on existing inter-city routes.

Improved transport services

So much for provision of new routes. Similar considerations apply to the organization of new or improved services on existing routes: the innovation tends to be first applied in areas where the existing demand is high, spreading into the less-rewarding regions at a later date. This has been clearly demonstrated in the case of omnibus services in Sweden. Godlund (1956) prepared maps of the routes served at selected years back to 1915 and in one case 1907. It is quite apparent how the first country routes to be exploited were those radiating from and connecting the more important centres and that the remoter and smaller places generating less traffic were brought into the system at a later date. Nor is the reason far to seek, for analysis of the financial returns showed a high positive correlation with the density of population in the territory served: the sparser the population, the lower the returns per vehicle–kilometre and vice versa. This is similar to the finding that milk collection costs are higher in areas of England and Wales in which but little milk is produced and lower where output is concentrated (page 104).

In his study of Wiltshire, Bracey (1952, 16) was struck by the

comprehensive development and high frequency of bus services in the valleys converging on Salisbury, in spite of the relatively low overall population density of Downland Wiltshire. These high frequencies have been encouraged by the linear settlement pattern, which offers a higher total population per 'bus mile' than obtains under less concentrated settlement.

Indeed, the post-war history of rural bus services in Britain is of a protracted fight against the reduction and abolition of services; the routes carrying the least traffic have been the most vulnerable, despite various forms of assistance that have been provided. Although a well-known phenomenon, the national pattern of contraction of bus services has not been as thoroughly documented as in the case of the railway system (Patmore 1966).

It will not have escaped the reader's attention that the above argument is nothing but the following proposition: that an area which is initially favoured, for whatever reason, tends to obtain the best communications first, which helps to reinforce the pre-existing relative advantage possessed by that region. In fact the analysis developed by Weber, Lösch and Isard, leading to the conclusion that agglomeration of urban-industrial activity is a proper and normal occurrence, also has its application in rural matters. Furthermore, there is an important element in the general case which appears to have been overlooked or not to have received the attention which it deserves. As far as it has been taken by Isard, the analysis which leads to the conclusion that the agglomeration of economic activity is the normal phenomenon is based upon the assumption that no innovation is introduced into a situation where techniques are assumed to remain constant. The conclusion is reinforced when account is taken of the factor discussed in the last few paragraphs, that an innovation in transport techniques tends to be first employed where there is already a high level of economic development and consequently a big demand for transport services. As new techniques are being developed at relatively frequent intervals, the main agglomerations tend to enjoy a succession of advantages and this must be a factor of some importance in maintaining the advantages of existing urban concentrations.

Further discussion of the agglomeration of agricultural settlements and land uses is reserved to the next chapter. To complete this one, a few remarks are warranted on the world distribution of rural population. These comments are not intended to elicit new facts or theories on the causes of high and low densities, but rather to point out that an important step in the argument which is commonly just assumed, and is hence little remarked, fits into the pattern of analysis developed in this book.

World distribution of rural population

There are many parts of the world in which a dense peasant population following a largely self-sufficient way of life has come into existence – the riverine lands of the lower Yangtze or Indus, for example. That such densities should be possible may be ascribed to many factors but the most important set of considerations is that, with the existing techniques employed, these areas offer the possibility of high yields on a sustained basis. Whereas a southern Japanese farming family may be able to live on the produce of less than one hectare of lowland soil, such a feat would be unthinkable in the mountainous interior of Hokkaido in the north, owing to the lower inherent fertility of these boreal lands.

Such reasoning is not complete. It states only that the more fertile lands are capable of *supporting* more persons per hectare of cultivated soil and says nothing as to *where* these people live. We have already seen (Chapter 3) that in certain circumstances agriculturalists live many kilometres from the lands which they regularly cultivate. Hence, it is conceivable that a Japanese family owning some fertile lowland patch might choose to live where the climate was pleasanter or the view more beautiful. Should sufficient families do just this, the paradoxical position would arise in which the more fertile area was the less densely peopled, though providing sustenance for persons living elsewhere. In a peasant society, this does not occur on anything but a local scale: defence against enemies, for example, is an important reason for villages being located on hilltops near the cultivated land. At the regional and world scale, it does not happen, for the reason that the prospective costs would be so enormous as to be insupportable. We have seen the handicap which is imposed by even 4 kilometres separating dwelling and field: distances much greater than this would mean such a deterioration in the productivity of both land and labour that it would be impossible to maintain existing populations with the techniques which they currently employ. The disadvantages of separation are multiplied enormously where it is necessary to guard crops against predatory beasts and birds, as in Africa and jungle areas generally, and where irrigation is practised or livestock kept.

The relationship between the capacity of the soil and the density of the population actually living on it operates only through the costs of separation, which are too great to be tolerated. Obvious, yes. But once stated, it is evident that in fact any analysis of the distribution of population in agricultural economies is an exercise in location concerned with the effects of overcoming distance.

8 Technical change

So far, the question of technical change has received only incidental notice. The method adopted in the previous chapters has been to consider situations in which, at the relevant time, the technical equipment employed was assumed to be unchanging. The idea of development has been conveyed mainly by the examination of a sequence of cases, each study relating to a point in time later than the previous one, as in Chapter 4. In this way, a number of the more obvious consequences of developments in transport and related techniques have been brought to light, notably the enlargement of the supply areas for the major urban concentrations of population, often also associated with population increase.

The purpose of this chapter is to draw together some of these threads and by working systematically to attempt to weave some additional designs. In so doing, attention will be directed mainly to what is happening at present and, where appropriate, an attempt will be made to indicate the significance of trends for the future. Theoretical analysis and study of the past and present may be justified for their own sake in the pursuit of knowledge. Where the findings have implications relevant to decisions which must be taken in the present or future, or merely for understanding what is happening and is likely to happen, then it is unsatisfactory to call a halt to the investigations, leaving it to others to make the predictions. The logic of the case which has been made in the previous chapters requires some glance at present and probable future trends.

A fundamental assumption must be made explicit. Any technical change creates conditions of disequilibrium, which may be of long or short duration according as the innovation in question is or is not major, and also according to the nature of the adjustment mechanism. However, in the absence of any other change we may assume that in time a new equilibrium will be achieved. In practice, of course, the *ceteris paribus* assumption does not hold and new events overtake each change. Thus, the most that can in fact be said is that after each technical change the relevant spatial system *tends* to a new equilibrium.

To avoid possible confusion, it should be noted that the discussion below relates mainly to the economically developed countries rather than the so-called underdeveloped ones. Thus, the analysis which is developed does not claim universal validity, though it seems likely that events happening in the United States and Western Europe now will find close parallels in the less advanced countries in future decades – or maybe generations. We begin with a discussion of technical changes affecting the farm and village scale of phenomenon and then proceed to regional and world matters.

Improved transport on the farm

The most striking recent innovation on the farm regarding modes of transport has been the tractor. First developed as a wheeled vehicle, the later introduction of track-laying or crawler tractors considerably widened the range of applications as a source of power for farming operations on sloping and heavy lands. The post-war period has also witnessed the development of miniature tractors and machines suitable for use on paddy rice lands. Wheeled vehicles in particular achieve relatively high speeds, which is invaluable for carting goods from one place to another. The rapid growth of the world's tractor fleet is indicated by the fact that in 1938–9 there were 3.6 million vehicles (the USSR excluded) whereas by 1964 there were 11.4 million, over three times the number and individually more powerful. By 1975, the fleet had grown to 14.9 million, with an additional 2.3 million in the USSR. At the same time, the number of horses, mules and asses – the chief draught animals – fell from 125.0 million in 1938–9 to 110.3 million in 1964–5, though since then numbers have remained much the same. Although in parts of Europe and North America mechanical power had very largely replaced draught animals by the early 1960s, for the world as a whole no more than one-fifth of the draught power used in agriculture was supplied by tractors, the rest being provided by animals and human labour (Grigg 1970); since 1960, the position has not in fact changed dramatically.

It would be wrong to suppose that ultimately the whole world will reach the position of Europe and North America, for farming conditions vary enormously. For example, it is only recently that small

Table 23 *Tractors in relation to agricultural area*

Region	Area in arable, permanent crops and permanent grass (million hectares)	Hectares of agricultural land per agricultural tractor		
	1975	1954	1964	1975
Europe	230	141	51	32
North and Central America	613	127	118	123
USSR	604	—	390	259
South America	548	2724	1008	945
Oceania	517	1641	1282	1181
Africa	1009	5945	3570	2536
Asia	1031	13 108	2673	817

Source: FAO, *Production Yearbook*, various issues

machines have been developed suitable for use on Japanese paddy lands, and it seems unlikely that tractors could ever be as important in terraced rice cultivation as in wheat production on the prairies and pampas.

Evidence collected by Razso (1959) gives a clear indication of the magnitude of the time savings implied by mechanization. For a variety of crops and farm commodities, he compared the tonnage that could be moved over specified distances by various means in one day. A tractor of 25 horse-power and drawing one trailer could move between three and four times the tonnage that could be shifted by an iron-wheeled horse-drawn cart over a distance of one kilometre; the ratio was generally nearer four to six for a haul of five kilometres.

More modest technical improvements can also have an enormous effect. Such may be the replacement of head porterage by mule or donkey, the use of a proper harness in place of the clumsy yoking of oxen by the horns, the employment of the faster horse instead of the lumbering ox, or the provision of inflatable rubber tyres instead of the metal rims on wooden wheels common to many carts. Early in the 1950s in the Italian commune of Borgo a Mozzano, remote in the mountains between Florence and Lucca, 95 per cent of goods were moved by human porterage and pack mules (Sorbi 1955). At much the same time, a survey of nearly 2000 lowland rice farms in the

Philippines showed that 31 per cent of the farmers consigned their rice to the local market by non-mechanical overland means – that is, by cart, pack animal, sledge and porter. In Visayas, the proportion was 67 per cent, in Mindanao 74 per cent and in Cagayan as much as 99 per cent (von Oppenfield *et al.* 1957). Richardson (1974) noted that the majority of Guyanese rice farmers walk to their fields at distances less than 4.0 kilometres. Between 4.0 and 8.8 kilometres, a mixture of modes is used (walking, cycling, animal and motor-vehicle); only at distances in excess of 8.8 kilometres is motorized transport the predominant means. Finally, in Colombia over half the nation's agricultural production leaves the farms on the backs of pack animals (Crossley 1972).

In contrast to these modest improvements, the application of aerial methods to many agricultural operations catches the imagination. Since the last world war, there has been a spectacular increase in such activities, including spraying, dressing, seeding, dropping rabbit poison in New Zealand and facilitating fence construction in otherwise inaccessible areas. Such has been the growth of this new technique that there is now a European Agricultural Aviation Centre at The Hague, issuing a quarterly journal. Undoubtedly aerial techniques are going to be of growing importance to farmers all over the world.

It is not possible to assess the total effect of innovations in diminishing the amount and cost of movement within the individual farm and to compare these savings with the economies in production achieved by other means. But it seems safe to aver that the benefits have been sufficiently great in relation to other developments, such as increases in yields, for the problem of transport within the farm to have declined in relative importance in the more advanced countries. In regions where mechanization is virtually complete, there may be relatively little scope for further reductions in the relative cost of transport on the farm, unless the expansion of aerial techniques continues. Elsewhere, a substantial drop in the relative cost of transport may be expected merely from the adoption of known techniques which are not at present widely used there. This relative decline in the importance of transport would seem to be likely even despite the spectacular increases in yields which can be obtained in some parts of the world from the application of simple devices like nitrogenous fertilizers.

External relations of settlements

When it comes to local transport external to the farm, the story is the same. The substitution of bicycles, motor-bicycles, cars and lorries for the more primitive methods has meant, or promises to mean, a substantial decline in the relative cost of transport. India is a clear case. In 1959, only 29 per cent of villages were within 2.4 kilometres of an all-weather road, and one-third were more than 8.8 kilometres distant. It is estimated that there are 12 million bullock carts in India, mostly used exclusively for agricultural operations and transport to local market centres. Whereas countries such as Britain, France, Japan and the United States have about 2.4 kilometres of farm-to-market roads for each square kilometre of cultivated land, in the Philippines the ratio is 0.6 and in India only 0.4. Nevertheless, with the spread of motorized transport in India, reducing transport costs to one-half or one-third, bullock carts still operate over a radius of 40 kilometres, whereas previously the limit was 80 (Owen 1968; see also Sen *et al.* 1971).

This important role of even quite simple innovations is evident from two studies in Africa. Writing of Zambia, Hellen (1968, 115) observed:

The humble bicycle was and is probably the most overworked and important machine in this part of Africa. It enables men to cycle hundreds of miles to work or to sell low weight articles like dried fish, caterpillars, grass mats and other manufactured items.

Indeed, within a radius of 16 kilometres around Jinja, Uganda, the greater part of the banana crop, a staple foodstuff, is moved by tradesmen on cycles (Whetham 1972).

Enormously important is the increase in personal mobility conferred by the possession of a bicycle or motor vehicle, which enables rural workers to live several kilometres or more from their place of work. The proportion of persons owning such means of locomotion is rising and undoubtedly will continue to rise, principally on account of improvements in the standard of living. Second and often overlooked is the fact that working hours are getting shorter in many parts of the world, with the consequence:

(1) That people have more time in which to travel, and
(2) Have more leisure to occupy, and hence greater social needs,

which encourages them to travel daily so that once at home these needs may be fulfilled.

At the same time as social needs are increasing, the capacity to satisfy them is also growing.

Reverting to a point made in Chapter 5, notice that an increasing number of services is being provided from without the farm and its farmstead. Electricity is one such. A study by the International Bank for Reconstruction and Development (1975) showed that in 1971 only 23 per cent of the rural and village population in Latin America was connected to electricity supplies, while in Asia the proportion was but 15 per cent and in Africa a mere 4 per cent. Water and sewerage are other services. In addition, articles such as bread, formerly made in the home, are now purchased from external sources. Thus, the external relations of farms and villages are assuming an increasing significance.

Perhaps pride of place in these external contacts should be given to education. In an illiterate peasant society the offspring are pressed into work of all kinds at a tender age, whether it be to watch the livestock or fetch water. When educational facilities are provided, and especially when schooling is made compulsory, the young must leave home daily. When the dwellings are gathered together, no child need travel very far but where there are dispersed settlements considerable distances may be involved. In Britain, the local authority is obliged, if so required, to provide transport when the journey exceeds 3.2 kilometres and this is a very costly service in the remoter rural areas. Over much of the world, children customarily travel several kilometres each way daily on foot. Clearly, this provides a strong incentive to live in or near a village with a school, to ease the burden of daily travel imposed on the children and also the parents if they transport their offspring.

The matter does not rest there. The shortage of teachers throughout the world is very grave and therefore attempts are being made to derive the maximum benefit from the staff that is available. One manifestation of this policy is the closure of the smaller rural schools all over Britain, bringing the children into larger units where they may be better grouped according to age and ability than is possible in the one- or two-teacher, all-age primary school. At the same time, the specialist skills of teachers are available to more pupils. Hence, the smaller villages are tending to lose their schools. Furthermore, where many parents are acutely conscious of the advantages conferred by a good education, there is a strong demand for a choice of facilities. A scantily peopled area cannot support more than one institution, so parents who are not satisfied with the local school must either face a long daily journey for their children, plus the possibility of considerable expense, or move house to a larger community.

Consequences

Manifold are the consequences of these developments (Clawson 1966). The most convenient approach is to discuss each major type of consequence arising from the interplay of all the considerations mentioned above. A reduction in the relative cost of movement within the farm means that when a farmer considers applying more labour, etc., to a distant field he has to reckon with a smaller cost on account of distance than formerly. The further away is the field, the greater will the saving be relative to other production costs. Thus, any decline in the relative cost of transport within the farm will mean that the level of gross and net output obtained from the land will diminish with distance less rapidly than before. This means that it becomes possible to intensify production over a greater part of the holding and the zoning of types and intensities of production will become less evident. Where the holding is sufficiently small, or the diminution in transport costs is adequately big, then zoning within the farm arising from the distance factor may well disappear. This will happen because the relative advantages of location become so small as hardly to matter, being outweighed by other considerations.

The point is admirably illustrated by the adoption of aerial techniques in the sheep-grazing areas of South Island, New Zealand. Holdings here are often hundreds, even thousands, of hectares in extent, frequently running up from the accessible plateaux to the broken lower mountain slopes. By aerial seeding and fertilizing and the dropping of fencing supplies, it has been possible to extend the area of intensive grazing into the formerly inaccessible parts of the holdings, helping substantially to increase wool and meat production. On a less spectacular scale, the same process operates widely over the world and is one factor among many leading to an increase in agricultural supplies and the raising of rural living standards.

The converse of this proposition is that, along with many other factors, it is possible for a given labour force, say a family, to cultivate a larger area than formerly. Or, in cultivating a given size of farm, a family can now dispense with hired labour. These aspects of the matter are more relevant for commercial, non-peasant economies where there are other occupations outside agriculture than they are for overpopulated peasant countries like China and India with a high level of rural un- and underemployment. In England and Wales, there is a steady trend towards larger farms. By 1974, the proportion of agricultural land in holdings of less than 8 hectares had fallen to only 1.8 per cent; at the same time, the relative significance of the larger farms has increased (Hirsch 1958; *Agricultural Statistics*). Altogether more important has been the exodus of labour from the land. As Table 24 shows, until 1951 the reduction was almost entirely due to the decline in wage labour whereas since then the number of farmers has also become substantially smaller, though not at the rate manifest for the decline in wage labour. Developments of a comparable nature have been occurring in Dutch agriculture, with the number of family and hired workers falling more rapidly than the number of farm operators (Bijkerk 1973). These trends do not arise solely from the considerations mentioned above, but nevertheless the diminution in the costs of transport within farms has contributed to the increase in farm size and exodus of rural labour.

Table 24 *England and Wales: persons occupied in agriculture* (*thousands*)

Year	Farmers	Relatives occupied on the farm	Contract workers on the farm	Others in agriculture	Total in agriculture
1851	249	112	1268	79	1708
1911	229	115	687	155	1186
1931	248	81	539	131	999
1951	263	88	483	132	966
1974	(209)*	68	192	71	540

* The number of *holdings*, which probably exceeds the number of farmers

Sources: Bellerby 1958 (for 1851 to 1951); *Agricultural Statistics* (for 1974)

An interesting, but minor, further consequence of this ability to intensify production up to the periphery of the holding relates to land consolidation. In preparing a scheme, it is normal for a survey to be carried out to establish the value of each parcel of land and so of each entire holding. On this basis, the new holdings are planned so that the farmers receive holdings which bear the same proportion to the new total value of farm land as the old ones did to the previous aggregate. In some cases, it may be necessary to make a cash adjustment where exact equity cannot otherwise be maintained. From the analysis which has been developed, it is quite evident that two adjacent parcels of land may be identical in every particular of natural endowment but, being situated on different farms at different distances from the farmsteads, have markedly different values to their owners. In the process of reallocation, they may well be given to some third person and their space-relationships with the new farmstead will differ from what they previously were. Clearly, it is a very tricky matter to make an accurate allowance for these changes in value, and in practice the matter appears to be very largely neglected. In so far as the technical changes which have been mentioned are applied, with a consequent general intensification of farming on the further plots, by so much is this problem of equity less important and the more justifiable it is to ignore the matter. Exactly the same argument applies to the assessment of land taxes.

It is becoming increasingly possible for the dwelling to be removed from the territory which is cultivated and in many respects such separation is becoming more desirable. One manifestation of this has already been noted; in the recent Dutch reclamation schemes, houses for wage workers are frequently built in the villages instead of adjacent to the farmstead. A similar movement is occurring in Britain, because of the increasing difficulty that owners have in letting to agricultural workers cottages which are isolated and hard to reach. Many of these, especially in southern England, are being taken over as weekend cottages by urban dwellers seeking to escape from bricks and mortar. To an increasing extent, agricultural wage workers live in villages and hamlets instead of dispersed dwellings. Much more extreme examples are reported from the United States, where two graphic but rather odd terms have come into use: 'suitcase' and 'sidewalk' farmers. The former are defined as persons who live more than 48 kilometres from the border of the county in which the land they cultivate lies. Frequently, such persons lead a migratory kind of existence, following the seasons at ploughing, planting and harvesting times, thereby providing extended use for the equipment they own. 'Sidewalk' farmers are those who live in nucleated settlements, cultivating land that may be some kilometres away (Kollmorgan and Jenks 1958). Although in the early 1950s it appeared that both forms of farm organization would continue to grow in relative importance, a later study by Hewes (1973) shows that in fact 'suitcase' farming has been in retreat since about 1950. This decline has resulted from the combination of problems over soil erosion, the government's post-war programme for taking land out of arable cultivation and having it put to grass, and the spread of irrigation and consequential change in farming practice. On the other hand, 'sidewalk' farming appears to be holding its own.

However, to keep some perspective on the experience of the United States, it is worth noting that in West Germany as a whole, 1.8 per cent of the urban labour force is occupied in farming and forestry; the proportion ranges from 2.9 per cent in the smaller towns (20–50 000 population) to 0.9 per cent in the cities of over 1.0 million inhabitants.

Much of the farm labor force in the cities is in commercial gardening, but the area occupied by commercial greenhouse and truck farming gardens is only a fraction of the total urban area utilized for farming and gardening. The greatest proportion of this land is true farmland and forests. Since the farmhouses are located in the cities, these urban farmers still commute to their fields not unlike their forefathers. [Holzner 1970, 331]

A significant further effect of reduced real transport costs is the increased degree of fragmentation of farm holdings that is made possible. In response to technical changes on the farm and the level of prices in the market place, farmers wish to enlarge their holdings. Only rarely is it possible to acquire land immediately adjacent to the existing holding; more usually, land must be rented or purchased at a distance. Thus, the proportion of land in non-contiguous holdings is rising in parts of the United States, and in some cases parcels of land may be as much as 40 kilometres away from the main plot (Smith 1975; Sublett 1975). This process of fragmentation by acquisition had begun by the mid 1800s but in the United States appears to have gathered momentum in recent decades. Sublett notes that the distance to non-contiguous arable land is about twice that to non-contiguous grass, i.e. the less intensively used is nearer. This probably reflects both variations in the quality of land and the fact that, in a dynamic situation of land acquisition, the greater marginal returns on arable land justify a higher outlay on transport.

Another contemporary development with important potential repercussions for the future is the growing interest in the efficiency with which birds and animals convert feeds into useful products – eggs, meat or milk. Such efficiency is achieved partly through careful breeding and partly by strictly controlled ingestion. Such control may preclude free ranging and often requires the animals or birds to be closely confined, all feed being brought to them. 'Broiler' chickens are an important case in point, but pigs are so treated and to an increasing extent veal calves and beef cattle are being reared by these methods. The conjunction of these new production techniques in animal husbandry and the transport improvements already noted indicates that it is becoming increasingly possible to separate the land from the dwellings and associated livestock facilities.

Great efforts have been directed towards the breeding of animals, principally cattle, capable of withstanding extreme conditions of heat. There has been considerable success, but one of the limiting factors is the provision of adequate fodder in tropical regions. Good breeding in the absence of good feeding is a waste of time. It appears that in the tropical and equatorial parts of the world adequate fodder can best be provided by special crops rather than improved ranges and this argues the advantages of stall-feeding in many cases. This is especially so in areas of intensive farming where much of the feed for livestock is the waste or residue of crops used in other ways. There is the further advantage with stall-feeding that the climatic environment of the beasts can be controlled to a greater or lesser extent. It may not be altogether fanciful to imagine that it will be more profitable to breed for high efficiency in the conversion of feed and to provide air-conditioning than to breed for high resistance to adverse climatic conditions. After all, the design of modern chicken houses and pig pens is, among other things, an exercise in the economical control of temperature, humidity and ventilation.

With irrigation, the problem is much less tractable. Only with the development of remote-controlled techniques for regulating the water supplies would it be possible for farmers to live away from their holdings. Since irrigated areas are commonly ones supporting a dense population, social intercourse and the provision of services are relatively easy for dispersed settlements. Hence the advantages of nucleation are much less apparent in this case.

Clearly, with the important exception of irrigation farming, there is a tendency which we may expect to continue for agricultural settlements to become increasingly nucleated or, in the terminology of location studies, agglomerated. At first sight, this appears to contradict the conclusion reached in Chapter 3 that a spontaneous dispersal is occurring widely over the world. The apparent discrepancy may be reconciled in the following way. First, that which is currently happening in a country such as the United Kingdom or United States – agglomeration – may not yet be appropriate for much poorer nations but is likely to become so with the passage of time. Second, where there has been an excessive concentration of the rural population into a few enormous settlements, some degree of dispersal is requisite if the farming is to be improved. The question really turns on the extent to which dispersal should take place; it would appear that in some cases placing the farmsteads on the holdings is going too far.

Here lies an acute problem in planning the layout of new settlements. Where the existing peasantry is poor, illiterate and unskilled in intensive forms of agriculture and lacks mechanical equipment, it is without question essential to locate the farmsteads on the holdings. However, this lays the foundations for an increase in wealth, better standards of education, more leisure, all forces which are likely to create conditions in which there is a growing desire to locate the dwellings in nucleated groups, a more pressing economic need to do so, and a greater ability to act upon these pressures. Should the layout conform to the initial needs, or the prospective ones? Or is a later change in the settlement pattern to be tolerated? Or what compromise solution should be adopted?

It is impossible to give a definitive answer to these questions. However, since it appears that the long-term trend is towards concentration of the rural populace, it is justifiable to argue that in any scheme for agricultural settlement the dwellings should be brought together into groups or villages to the maximum extent that, in the light of particular circumstances, can be tolerated. In this way, the longer-term problems of adjustment may be minimized and the maximum concession is made to a feeling common among persons accustomed to living in nucleated settlements, that they do not at first like the loneliness of living in dispersed dwellings.

Last among the consequences to be noted at the small scale but by no means the least important is that, in so far as the distribution of production within the farm is less dependent upon location with respect to the farmstead, it must become relatively more affected by other factors. In practice, these are the conditions of the natural environment. To an increasing extent, crops can be grown on the land which is best suited to give a high yield of good quality, yet another factor working towards an increase in yields and a general improvement in the productivity of both land and labour. This argument will be developed more fully in the context of the larger scales, the region and the world, and all that is here necessary is to note that a phenomenon which is chiefly significant at the larger scale is also apparent at the smaller.

Cheaper transport

Let us, then, turn to the wider view and look first at the cheapening of transport. There are three major ways in which transport costs have become and are becoming less in relation to the value of goods:

(1) The substitution of improved means of transport for more rudimentary methods.

(2) Improvements within individual transport media.

(3) The greater degree of processing undergone by products and changes in the type of product towards the more valuable ones.

In the next few paragraphs each will be examined in turn.

The spread of new transport techniques – whether stage-coach, canal, railway, motor vehicles, steam and diesel ships, or aeroplanes – yields savings in transport costs which are sufficiently great and widespread to be obvious. There is no need to argue the case and it will suffice to give one or two illustrations to show how great the savings may be. De Foville, writing in 1880, quoted the following approximate figures in French francs per metric-tonne kilometre:

	Francs	*Cents*
Porter	3	33
Muleteer	–	87
Camel caravan	–	48
Carriages, seventeenth century, at 1880 prices	1	50
Carriages, nineteenth century	–	20
Railways, early nineteenth century	–	25
Railways, 1870s	–	6

A modern example comes from Kenya, where porters or donkeys carried goods in the northern coastal belt at $1.0–1.75 per ton mile.

With the opening of a road in 1953, motor trucks handled this traffic at between 50 and 75 cents per ton mile (Hance 1958).

The reader who seeks more ample documentation of the potential savings in transport costs in the less developed parts of the world is referred to Clark and Haswell (1970). These authors collected a large array of data, which show that the orders of magnitude quoted above are realistic. In addition, one may note Gould (1960) for Ghana early in the present century; Harbison (1970) and Felstehausen (1971) for Colombia, respectively in the late nineteenth and early twentieth centuries, and contemporaneously; and Taylor (1951), Chinitz (1960) and Fogel (1964) for the United States in the nineteenth and twentieth centuries; and Hawke (1970) for England and Wales in the nineteenth century.

When it comes to changes within a single medium of transport, the problems of measurement become acute. At the time the first edition of this book was published in 1962, relatively few studies had appeared measuring changes in transport costs relative to other prices, and therefore it then seemed necessary to present some detailed evidence showing how, during the nineteenth and twentieth centuries, real transport costs by particular modes had declined. Since then, the proliferation of productivity studies has rendered it unnecessary to rehearse the findings in detail. For the United States, the productivity of the transport sector as a whole and of the individual modes rose faster than productivity in the other major sectors of the economy, over the period from about 1890 to the mid 1950s (Barger 1951; Mansfield 1965; Fishlow 1966). Mansfield's data indicate that transport productivity rose at 3.1 per cent annually, compared with a 1.7 per cent growth in the economy as a whole. The more recent study by Deakin and Seward (1969) for the United Kingdom indicates a continuation of the trend.

There can be no doubt that over the hundred years to about 1950 or 1960, technical innovation and changes in traffic conditions allowed the transport industries to outstrip most others in efficiency gains, thus realizing a sustained and sizeable decline in the real cost of transport mode by mode. However, it appears that this general decline in the real costs may not continue in the future; it seems more plausible to suggest that overall productivity gains in transport will roughly match the more general gains in efficiency. Nevertheless, there is still a great deal of scope for lowering costs locally by the application of known technology. A major example is the opening of the St Lawrence Seaway in 1959, following which freight rates to the interior littoral of North America were reduced substantially. The more recently completed road tunnel under Mont Blanc, connecting France and Italy, provides the first all-season road connection over the Alps between the two nations. Yet other cases are the lakes formed behind the Kainji Dam and on the Volta river, both providing large expanses of navigable water.

The third manner in which transport costs are declining in relative importance arises from the changing nature of agricultural produce. As living standards rise, dietary habits change, leading to an increase in the relative importance of foods like meat, dairy produce, fruit and vegetables, which tend to replace the staple foodstuffs of grains and tubers. These higher-class foods are more difficult to transport than are crops like wheat, being more perishable; but their much higher value in relation to bulk means that relatively speaking the cost of transport is lower. To the extent that dietary habits continue to change in the direction which has so far been apparent in the more advanced countries, there will be a decline in the significance of transport in agriculture. Second, and working in the same direction, is the increasing extent to which foodstuffs are processed. This may take the simple form of washing potatoes or carrots on the farm prior to dispatch to market, or it may be the growing popularity of pre-cooked and frozen foods. In such cases, the value of the commodity is raised without adding materially to transport costs.

Consequences

Jumper (1974) states that approximately two-thirds of the price paid by American consumers of agricultural produce are attributable to marketing costs; for fresh vegetables, the proportion is 80 per cent. Transport costs form only a part, though a major part, of marketing costs. Thus, any diminution in the real cost of transport may be expected to have a significant impact on agricultural location patterns, a fact recognized explicitly as long ago as 1855 by Lardner, and indeed von Thünen.

One consequence has already been noted in Chapter 4. Where either population (hence demand) is growing, or transport costs are falling in real terms, or both are happening simultaneously, an expansion of supply zones will occur, with possibly intensification of agriculture in the hither zones. In Chapter 4, this process was viewed as if from the 'central city', as an expansion in the supply area. If our viewpoint is that of any one parcel of land, then the process will be apparent as changing patterns of production on the farm. As Schlebecker (1960, 203) remarked of America: 'On a single farm a man might in his own lifetime be in cattle country, wheat country, corn country, and dairy country.' The outward expansion of the crop zones is locally manifest as a succession of enterprises, following a time-sequence from less to more intensive. (See also Bressler and King 1970.) This very point was in fact made as long ago as 1918 (Wolff) in his examination of the plight of British agriculture; he urged the farming community to recognize the 'natural order of things' and to adjust by switching products and generally intensify agriculture, to exploit the opportunities created by the expansion of the inner zone of intensive production. Changes of this kind have been most easily recognized in the temperate grasslands opened to settlement in the nineteenth century, but are also well documented for other times and places (see page 87). A contemporary example of the *visible* evidence of intensification following a reduction in transport costs comes from Colombia; Crist and Nissly (1973, 50) report how the provision of road access eastwards from Bogota enabled milk and cheese to be marketed, with the result that 'previously unused boundaries between fields, a yard or so wide, are now planted in silage grasses for stall feeding of milk cows'.

A closely related phenomenon is that of an increase in the degree of regional specialization. This arises in the following manner. With a decline in transport costs, the advantage conferred by proximity to markets and to inputs diminishes in absolute importance. Consequently, other location factors must assume a larger relative significance, principally conditions of climate, soil and topography. Collectively, these have a big effect upon the earliness of the crop season and thus on the price which can be obtained for the produce and on the costs of production. The consequence is that instead of a particular crop being grown near the consuming centres and necessarily under very diverse physical conditions, it is increasingly possible for it to be grown in a limited number of places which physically are well suited to its requirements. The advantages of lower production costs and/or earlier season are not fully absorbed by transport costs, as previously they were.

Baker discussed the matter at some length as long ago as 1921, drawing attention to the influence of topography, soil fertility moisture and temperature. What Baker called regional 'specialization' of production may also be termed regional 'agglomeration' of enterprises, for if production is locally concentrated so also must producers be congregated together. The agglomeration of like enterprises at the regional level may be compared with the agglomeration of dwellings into nucleated settlements discussed earlier in this chapter – a similar phenomenon but affecting a different element of the agricultural economy.

We have already examined some evidence that supports this conclusion (chapter 4). Attention should also be given to the study by Leaman and Conkling (1975). Their study area lies south of, but bordering, Lake Ontario. In 1840, the Erie Canal had yet to be opened but by 1860 it had been in use for fifteen years; the two decades also saw the advent of the railways. The overall effect of these innovations was to halve transport costs. Hence, the authors hypothesized, agriculture should become better adjusted to the local variations in environmental conditions. Using fairly sophisticated statistical techniques, the authors found that indeed this process could be detected. At a quite different scale, Symons and White (1975) noted the emergence of regional specialization in grain production in the USSR in the period of approximately 1851–1881; specialization was conceived in terms of production surpluses and deficits, and the emergence of regional specialization was attributed to the construction of the railway system.

Several other factors are working in the same direction, encouraging local specialization of production but differing in importance from product to product. One of the outstanding developments in the retailing trade of fresh food in the United Kingdom since the last war, following the lead of the United States, has been the expansion of business handled by the big chain stores, such as Marks & Spencer. Organizations of this kind require large quantities of standardized produce. But graded and branded goods are of increasing importance in the trade of other shops, notably the self-service establishments. This development demands either that production be on a large scale or that the output of numerous small holdings should pass through a single grading and packing centre, such as a co-operative. In the latter case, there are self-evident advantages in having a number of producers close together, especially if the central organization also supplies farming requisites. The establishment of Home Grown Fruits, Ltd, in 1961, to grade and market between one-quarter and one-third of the commercial apple crop in Britain produced by only 300 growers (*The Times* 26 September 1963) is an example that provides some parallels with the earlier evolution of hop production and marketing in Kent (Harvey 1963). Since there seems to be every likelihood that standardized branded produce will take an increasing share of the market, there will be a continuing pressure towards local specialization.

Closely related to the above is the ability of large organizations to bargain for favourable transport rates. One of the classic cases is that of California in the United States; this state managed to establish itself early as the major supplier of the east coast for many types of fruit and vegetable and, because of the large scale of shipments, was able to obtain favourable treatment from the railways. Florida found it difficult to break into the market, having initially a low level of production and therefore being unable to get such good freight rates. Road transport has given Florida its chance, because there appear to be few economies of scale in road transport operations (Harrison 1963) and consequently the small scale of production in the beginning was much less of a handicap.

Third, production techniques in all types of agricultural enterprise are getting more and more elaborate, requiring a greater degree of technical knowledge and skill. It is more difficult for each farmer to keep abreast of developments, even if he has the ability and the interest to follow events closely. Increasingly do farmers have to rely upon outside guidance and advice, whether this be provided by the official National Agricultural Advisory Service or firms selling agricultural necessities. With specialist types of production, which are becoming more and more important, specialized information is needed, and this can be and is most effectively provided where particular types of enterprise are locally concentrated. Elsewhere, the standard of service is inevitably poorer. It is becoming increasingly common for the smaller producers to hire the services of contracting firms or the use of particular pieces of machinery. When the equipment is specialized, it is evidently going to be easier and cheaper to arrange such services where there is a reasonable demand which will keep the machinery in use than where the demand is sporadic and small.

The fourth factor of importance is the growing scale of factory manufacturing and processing operations. Scale increases arise from technical developments in plant and equipment and the rationalization of production processes. To the extent that scale economies outweigh increases in transport costs, and also to the extent that agricultural produce is factory processed, a continuous evolution of location patterns can be expected. In this evolution, we may expect to see evidence of localization of production. The British sugar-beet industry is a case in point. In recent years, the total area in beet has stabilized. Meantime, scale economies in sugar processing have been realized. As a result, 1972 saw the first closure of a sugar-beet factory – the only factory in Scotland, at Cupar. The second closure was at Selby in 1974, matched by an equivalent expansion in factory capacity at York. The prospect is that the process will continue, resulting in a more localized pattern of sugar-beet production (Watts 1974). This process will be especially important where the raw product is highly perishable (like tea), is very bulky and loses much weight in processing (as in the case of butter and cheese), or yields a waste product which is returned to many of the farms (for example, the pulp yielded by sugar beet). These characteristics may be present in various combinations. Since there is every prospect that technical development will produce further scale economies in processing, there will be a continuing tendency for the output of particular items to be gathered round a limited number of factories.

Reverting for a moment to the effects of a cheapening of transport in encouraging a greater degree of local specialization of production, there is a seeming paradox which warrants attention. Brinkmann (Benedict 1935) observed that in some areas a lowering of transport costs could lead to a diversification of the agricultural economy. The reasoning behind this conclusion is as follows. Imagine an area which is inherently capable of producing several products, but is so situated with respect to markets as to be at the extensive margin of cultivation, finding only one crop yields a sufficient return to be worth growing. Under these conditions, monoculture must necessarily occur. If real transport costs become less, one or more of the enterprises which potentially could be engaged is brought within the ambit of possibilities. Under conditions of perfect adjustment, this might merely mean the replacement of one type of monoculture by another, as the production zones expand. But since adjustment never is perfect, farmers will have the choice of two or more crops, differences in the profitability of which are too small to bother about. Mixed farming is then likely to occur. It is, however, probable, even if there are marked differences in the profitability of the individual products, that farmers will choose mixed cultivation for at least three reasons:

(1) The combination of products will probably mean a net increase in yields and hence in the net profit of the farm as a whole.

(2) If one crop fails in any year, another may survive or even be highly successful. This helps to increase the stability of the farm income.

(3) There is likely to be a better distribution of work throughout the year and therefore a more economical use of labour and machinery.

While an increasing degree of regional specialization is the general trend, this is quite compatible with some change towards diversification at the extensive margin of cultivation as it ceases to be the margin.

The evidence and arguments so far presented have all tended in one direction, to the conclusion that agglomeration is likely to become increasingly important. There is one important set of circumstances which appears to be working in the opposite direction. Schultz (1951) and Price (1953) have observed that the payments which are made for the use of land, or rent, are becoming a smaller proportion of the expenses of agriculture in the more advanced countries. Price adduces two reasons for this: first, that agricultural production is being intensified generally; second, that there is a growing proportion of intensively farmed products, a shift from wheat to poultry, from potatoes to dairy produce. Both trends imply an increasing use of fertilizers, machinery, sprays, etc.: this means that the inherent qualities of the soil are becoming progressively less important for agricultural production. We would not, then, expect agglomeration of production into areas which are well suited physically.

Price omits to consider that some of the decline in the importance of rent arises from a third factor, that which we have been considering. With improved means of communication, the importance of location with respect to the market has diminished and this causes a reduction in the relative importance of rent (Chisholm 1961). Thus, the decline in the relative importance of land in the operations of agriculture attributable to the increasing use of other inputs is less than is suggested by Schultz and Price.

The second point to notice is that in most countries, or very large sections of them, the price which a farmer has to pay for manufactured inputs does not vary at all from place to place, or only very slightly. Manufacturers of machinery in particular tend to fix a uniform price throughout their sales area in a country and the same is true for most other requisites except the most bulky. Where regional price variations do occur, as between countries, they tend to be fairly small, because the cost of transport on manufactured goods is not proportionately very great. It therefore happens that whereas location has a very big effect upon the price which a farmer receives for his produce, it has a much lesser effect upon the costs of his inputs of machinery, fertilizers and buildings (Chisholm 1966). Reinforcing this contrast is the habit of many trades unions of bargaining for national wage levels; in the United Kingdom the agreed minimum rates of pay for agricultural workers are uniform throughout the country.

With changes in the cost-structure of agriculture, especially towards the use of more equipment and fertilizer, there is a growing proportion of the total costs of production which are uninfluenced by location or are influenced to only a small extent. Thus, it is entirely compatible to argue that while the physical qualities of the land – soil, slope, climate etc. – are becoming less important in relation to all the factors influencing the profits of farming, nevertheless among those factors which vary in quality or price from one place to another the physical environment is assuming more significance. The physical environment is therefore playing a bigger part in determining the location of production.

The conclusion is inescapable. At all scales, in the economically more advanced nations, powerful economic forces are working for an increasing degree of agglomeration. This is not to say that these constraints are ineluctable; where, for a variety of reasons, such tendencies towards centralization and specialization are regarded as undesirable, action can be taken to redress the 'imbalance'. Such action will be motivated by social and political needs and it may be entirely legitimate that these should have precedence over economic considerations. This is not the place to take up these wider issues. My purpose will have been achieved if such decisions are informed by a fuller understanding of the economic forces which operate to mould the geography of the world.

Bibliography

VAN AARTSEN, J. P. (1944), 'Land classification in relation to its agricultural value: a review of systems applied', *International Review of Agriculture*, July–August and November–December

ADELMAN, I., and G. DALTON (1971), 'Modernisation in village India', *Economic Journal*, vol. 81, pp. 563–79

AGARWAL, S. K. (1971), *The Economics of Land Consolidation in India*, S. Chand

AGRICULTURAL DEVELOPMENT AND ADVISORY SERVICE, MAFF (1973), 'Agriculture in the urban fringe', *Technical Report* no. 30, MAFF

AHMAD, E. (1952), 'Rural settlement types in the Uttar Pradesh (United Provinces of Agra and Oudh)', *Annals*, Association of American Geographers, vol. 42, pp. 223–46

AKINOLA, R. A. (1964), 'The Ibadan region', *Journal*, Geographical Association of Nigeria, vol. 6, pp. 102–15

ALBION, R. G. (1926), *Forests and Sea Power: The Timber Problem of the Royal Navy 1652–1862*, Harvard University Press

ALLAN, W. (1965), *The African Husbandman*, Oliver & Boyd

ALONSO, W. (1964), *Location and Land Use: Toward a General Theory of Land Rent*, Harvard University Press

ANCEY, G. (1974), *Relations de voisinage ville–campagne. Une analyse appliquée à Bouaké: sa couronne et sa région (Côte d'Ivoire)*, Orstrom

ANDREWS, D., and N. B. LILWALL (1974), 'Scale and diversification economies in fruit and vegetable freezing', *Bulletin* no. 10, East of Scotland College of Agriculture, Economics and Farm Management Department

APTHORPE, R., and J. MACARTHUR (1968), 'Land settlement policies in Kenya', in R. Apthorpe (ed.), *Land Settlement and Rural Development in Eastern Africa*, Transition Books, 29–32

ATKINS, P. J. (1977a), 'London's intra-urban milk supply, *circa*

1790–1914', *Transactions*, Institute of British Geographers, New Series, vol. 2, pp. 383–99

ATKINS, P. J. (1977*b*), *The Milk Trade of London* c. *1790–1914*, unpublished Ph.D. thesis, University of Cambridge

BAKER, A. R. H., and R. A. BUTLIN (eds.) (1973), *Studies in Field Systems in the British Isles*, Cambridge University Press

BAKER, O. E. (1921), 'The increasing importance of the physical conditions in determining the utilization of land for agricultural and forest production in the United States', *Annals*, Association of American Geographers, vol. 11, pp. 17–46

BAKER, S. (1973), *Milk to Market: Forty Years of Milk Marketing*, Heinemann

BARGER, H. (1951), *The Transportation Industries 1889–1946: A Study of Output, Employment and Productivity*, National Bureau of Economic Research

VAN BATH, B. H. S. (1963), *The Agrarian History of Western Europe A D 500–1850*, Arnold

BELLERBY, J. R. (1958), 'The distribution of manpower in agriculture and industry 1851–1951', *Farm Economist*, vol. 9, pp. 1–11

BENEDICT, E. T. (ed.) (1935), *Theodor Brinkmann's Economics of the Farm Business*, University of California Press

BERESFORD, M. W., and J. K. ST JOSEPH (1958), *Medieval England: An Aerial Survey*, Cambridge University Press

BERLER, A. (1970), *Urban-Rural Relations in Israel: Social and Economic Aspects*, Settlement Study Centre, Rehovet

BHATTACHARYA, C. G., and P. N. POTAKEY (1969), *A Study of Cocoa Farming and Cocoa Farmers in the Eastern Region of Ghana Using an Integrated Household Survey*, Institute of Statistical, Social and Economic Research, University of Ghana (mimeo)

BIJHOUWER, J. T. P. (1949), 'Kavelmaten hier en elders', *Landbouwkundig Tijdschrift*

BIJKERK, C. (1973), 'Rural development in the Netherlands', Institute for Land and Water Management Research, Wageningen (mimeo)

BIROT, P., and J. DRESCH (1953), *La Méditerranée et le Moyen-Orient*, vol. 1, Presses Universitaires de France

BLAIKIE, P. M. (1971), 'Spatial organization of agriculture in some north Indian villages, Part I', *Transactions*, Institute of British Geographers, vol. 52, pp. 1–40

BOAL, F. W. (1970), 'Urban growth and land value patterns: government influences', *Professional Geographer*, vol. 22, pp. 79–82

BONNEY, R. S. P. (1964), *The Relationship between Road Building and Economic and Social Development in Sabah*, Road Research Laboratory, 3 vols. (mimeo)

BORCHERT, G. (1967), 'Die Wirtschaftsräume Angolas. Transportprobleme und Rentabilätsgrenzen der Produktion', *Hamburger Beiträge zur Afrika-kunde*, vol. 6, Deutsches Institut für Afrika-Forschung

BOURRIÈRES, P. (1950), 'Essai d'étude économique générale des voies de communication en pays neuf', *Annales des Ponts et Chaussées*, in various parts

BOURRINET, J. (1971), *Coût de transport et d'exportation des produits agricoles*, Éditions Cujas

BRACEY, H. E. (1952), *Social Provision in Rural Wiltshire*, Methuen

BRADING, D. A. (1971), *Miners and Merchants in Bourbon Mexico 1763–1810*, Cambridge University Press

BRESSLER, R. G., and R. A. KING (1970), *Markets, Prices, and Interregional Trade*, Wiley

BRITTON, D. K. (1969), *Cereals in the United Kingdom: Production, Marketing and Utilisation*, Pergamon

BROOKFIELD, H. C. (1968), 'New directions in the study of agricultural systems in Tropical areas', in E. T. Drake (ed.), *Evolution and Environment*, Yale University Press, pp. 413–39

BROOKFIELD, H. C. (1969), 'The environment as perceived', in C. Board *et al.* (eds.), *Progress in Geography*, vol. 1, Arnold, pp. 51–80

BROOKFIELD, H. C. (1973), 'Full circle in Chimbu. A study of trends and cycles', in H. C. Brookfield (ed.), *The Pacific in Transition: Geographical Perspectives on Adaptation and Change*, Arnold, pp. 127–60

BROOKFIELD, H. C., and D. HART (1971), *Melanesia: A Geographical Interpretation of an Island World*, Methuen

BROWN, A. J. (1969), 'Surveys in applied economics: regional economics, with special reference to the United Kingdom', *Economic Journal*, vol. 79, pp. 759–96

BROWN, J. A., and S. S. SALKIN (1974), 'Underemployment in South Vietnam: a comment and a discussion of family labour', *Economic Development and Cultural Change*, vol. 23, pp. 151–60

BUCK, J. L. (1937), *Land Utilization in China*, Oxford University Press

BULL, G. B. G. (1956), 'Thomas Milne's land utilization map of the London area in 1800', *Geographical Journal*, vol. 122, pp. 25–30

CARLSON, A. W. (1975), 'Long-lots in the Rio Arriba', *Annals, Association of American Geographers*, vol. 65, pp. 48–57

CHARSLEY, S. (1968), 'The group farm scheme in Uganda', in R. Apthorpe (ed.), *Land Settlement and Rural Development in Eastern Africa*, Transition Books, pp. 57–64

CHINITZ, B. (1960), *Freight and the Metropolis. The Impact of America's Transport Revolutions on the New York Region*, Harvard University Press

CHISHOLM, M. (1957), 'Regional variations in road transport costs: milk collection from farms in England and Wales', *Farm Economist*, vol. 8, pp. 30–8

CHISHOLM, M. (1961), 'Agricultural production, location and rent', *Oxford Economic Papers*, vol. 13, pp. 342–59

CHISHOLM, M. (1966), *Geography and Economics*, Bell

CHISHOLM, M. (1968), *Rural Settlement and Land Use: An Essay in Location*, 2nd edition, Hutchinson

CHISHOLM, M. (1971), 'Freight transport costs, industrial location and regional development', in M. Chisholm and G. Manners (eds.), *Spatial Policy Problems of the British Economy*, Cambridge University Press, pp. 213–44

CHISHOLM, M., and P. O'SULLIVAN (1973), *Freight Flows and Spatial Aspects of the British Economy*, Cambridge University Press

CHRISTALLER, W. (1966), *Central Places in Southern Germany*, Prentice-Hall (translated by C. W. Baskin)

CLARK, C., and M. HASWELL (1970), *The Economics of Subsistence Agriculture*, 4th edition, Macmillan

CLARKE, D. L. (1968), *Analytical Archaeology*, Methuen

CLARKE, D. L. (1977), *Spatial Archaeology*, Academic Press

CLARKE, W. C. (1971), *Place and People. An Ecology of a New Guinean Community*, University of California Press

CLAWSON, M. (1966), 'Factors and forces affecting the optimum future rural settlement pattern in the United States', *Economic Geography*, vol. 42, pp. 283–93

CLAWSON, M. (1971), *Suburban Land Conversion in the United States: an Economic and Governmental Process*, Johns Hopkins University Press

CONSTANDSE, A. K. (1957), 'L'aménagement d'un polder aux Pays-

Bas: problèmes sociaux et démographiques', *Population*, vol. 12, pp. 401–12

CONSTANDSE, A. K. (1974), private communication

COOLMAN, F., and H. WILLEMS (1960), 'Mechanization and the small farm', in J. L. Meij (ed.), *Mechanization in Agriculture*, North Holland

COPPOCK, J. T. (1971), *An Agricultural Geography of Great Britain*, Bell

CRIST, R. E., and C. M. NISSLY (1973), *East from the Andes. Pioneer Settlements in the South American Heartland*, University of Florida Press

CROSSLEY, J. C. (1972), 'Continuing obstacles to agricultural development in Latin America', *Journal of Latin American Studies*, vol. 4, pp. 293–305

DARBY, H. C. (1936), 'The economic geography of England, AD 1000–1250', in H. C. Darby (ed.), *Historical Geography of England before 1800*, Cambridge University Press

DEAKIN, B. M., and T. SEWARD (1969), *Productivity in Transport: A Study of Employment, Capital, Output, Productivity and Technical Change*, Cambridge University Press for University of Cambridge, Department of Applied Economics

DEFOE, D. (1948), *A Tour through England & Wales*, Everyman

DEMANGEON, A. (1926), 'Problèmes actuels et aspects nouveaux de la vie rurale en Égypte', *Annales de Géographie*, vol. 35, pp. 155–73

DEMANGEON, A. (1947), *Problèmes de géographie humaine*, 3rd edition, Armand Colin

DOUIE, J. M. (1915), *Punjab Settlement Manual*, The Superintendent, Government Printing, Punjab

DOVRING, F. (1965a), *Land and Labour in Europe in the Twentieth Century*, 3rd edition, Heinemann

DOVRING, F. (1965b), 'The transformation of European agriculture', in H. J. Habakkuk and M. M. Postan (eds.), *The Cambridge Economic History of Europe*, vol. 6, part 2, Cambridge University Press, pp. 603–72

DOWNS, R. M., and D. STEA (eds.) (1973), *Image and Environment. Cognitive Mapping and Spatial Behaviour*, Arnold

DRAISMA, M. (1958), *Teelt en Bemesting op Bouwland in de Practijk*, Ministerie van Landbouw (*Cultivation and Fertilisation of Field Crops as Practised in the Netherlands*, with a summary in English)

DUBY, G. (1962), *Rural Economy and Country Life in the Medieval West*, Arnold

DUMONT, R. (1957), *Types of Rural Economy*, Methuen

DUNN, E. S. Jr. (1954), *The Location of Agricultural Production*, University of Florida Press

DUNSDORFS, E. (1956), *The Australian Wheat-Growing Industry, 1788–1948*, University Press, Melbourne

VAN DUSSELDORP, D. B. W. M. (1971), *Planning of Service Centres in Rural Areas of Developing Countries*, International Institute for Land Reclamation, Wageningen

EAST AFRICA ROYAL COMMISSION (1955), *Report*, Cmd 9475, HMSO

EAST, G. (1937), 'Land utilization in England at the end of the eighteenth century', *Geographical Journal*, vol. 89, pp. 156–72

EAST, W. G. (1956), *An Historical Geography of Europe*, 4th edition, Methuen

EDWARDS, D. (1961), *An Economic Study of Small Farming in Jamaica*, University College of the West Indies

EDWARDS, S. L. (1969), 'Transport costs in the wholesale trades', *Journal of Transport Economics and Policy*, vol. 3, pp. 272–8

EDWARDS, S. L. (1970), 'Transport cost in British industry', *Journal of Transport Economics and Policy*, vol. 4, pp. 1–19

EIDT, R. C. (1971), *Pioneer Settlement in Northeast Argentina*, University of Wisconsin Press

ELLISON, A., and J. HARRISS (1972), 'Settlement and land use in the prehistory and early history of Southern England; a study based on locational models', in D. L. Clarke (ed.), *Models in Archaeology*, Methuen, pp. 911–62

ELY, R. T., and G. S. WEHRWEIN (1940), *Land Economics*, Macmillan

ENYEDI, GY. (1976), *Hungary. An Economic Geography*, Westview Press (translation by M. Völgyes)

EUROPEAN ECONOMIC COMMUNITY (1977), *Newsletter on the Common Agricultural Policy*, no. 3

EWALD, U. (1977), 'The von Thünen principle and agricultural zonation in colonial Mexico', *Journal of Historical Geography*, vol. 3, pp. 123–33

EYRE, J. D. (1959), 'Sources of Tokyo's fresh food supply', *Geographical Review*, vol. 49, pp. 455–74

FALQUE, M. (1973), 'Vers une nouvelle fonction de l'agriculture périurbaine', *Études Rurales*, vols. 49–50, pp. 69–96

FELSTEHAUSEN, H. (1971), 'Planning problems in improving Colombian roads and highways', *Land Economics*, vol. 47, pp. 1–13

FENNELL, R. (1977), private communication, from Institute of Agricultural Economics, Oxford

FISHER, F. J. (1934–5), 'The development of the London food market, 1540–1640', *Economic History Review*, vol. 5, pp. 46–64

FISHLOW, A. (1965), *American Railroads and the Transformation of the Ante-Bellum Economy*, Harvard University Press

FISHLOW, A. (1966), 'Productivity and technological change in the railroad sector, 1840–1910', in National Bureau of Economic Research, *Output, Employment and Productivity in the United States after 1800*, Columbia University Press, pp. 583–646

FLORENCE, P. S. (1944), 'The selection of industries suitable for dispersion into rural areas', *Journal*, Royal Statistical Society, vol. 107, pp. 93–107

FOGEL, R. W. (1964), *Railroads and American Economic Growth: Essays in Econometric History*, Johns Hopkins Press

FOOD AND AGRICULTURE ORGANIZATION (1971), *Report on the 1960 World Census of Agriculture*, vol. 5, FAO

FOOD AND AGRICULTURE ORGANIZATION (1976), *Progress in Land Reform. Sixth Report*, FAO

FOUND, W. C. (1971), *A Theoretical Approach to Rural Land-use Patterns*, Arnold

DE FOVILLE, A. (1880), *La Transformation des moyens de transport et ses conséquences économiques et sociales*

FRAZER, R. (1973), 'The Fijian village and the independent farmer', in H. C. Brookfield (ed.), *The Pacific in Transition: Geographical Perspectives in Adaptation and Change*, Arnold, pp. 75–96

GALIZZI, G. (1964), *Localizzazione della Produzione Agricola*, Giuffre

GALLOWAY, J. H. (1968), 'The sugar industry of Pernambuco during the nineteenth century', *Annals*, Association of American Geographers, vol. 58, pp. 285–303

GAMBLE, C. (1978), 'Resource exploitation and the spatial patterning of hunter-gatherers: a case study', in D. Green *et al.*, *Social Organization and Settlement. Contributions from anthropology, archaeology and geography*, British Archaeological Reports, International Series (Supplementary), vol. 47 (i), pp. 153–85

GANEWATTE, P. (1974), 'Fragmentation of paddy land. A case study of five purana villages in Anuradhapura District', *Occasional Publication Series*, no. 5, Agrarian Research and Training Institute, Colombo

GILBOY, E. W. (1934), *Wages in Eighteenth Century England*, Harvard University Press

GILG, J.-P. (1970). 'Culture commerciale et discipline agraire obadéné (Tchad)', *Études Rurales*, vols. 37–38–39, pp. 173–97

GLAMANN, K. (1971), *European Trade 1500–1750*, Fontana

GLAMANN, K. (1977), 'The changing patterns of trade', in E. E. Rich and C. H. Wilson (eds.), *The Cambridge Economic History of Europe, Volume 5: The Economic Organization of Early Modern Europe*, Cambridge University Press, pp. 185–289

GLOVER, D. R., and J. L. SIMON (1975), 'The effect of population density on infrastructure: the case of road building', *Economic Development and Cultural Change*, vol. 23, pp. 453–68

GODLUND, S. (1956), 'Bus service in Sweden', *Lund Studies in Geography*, Series B, no. 17

GOOD, C. M. (1970), *Rural Markets and Trade in East Africa*, Research Paper 128, Department of Geography, University of Chicago

GOODLAND, R. J. A., and H. S. IRWIN (1975), *Amazon Jungle: Green Hell to Red Desert?*' Elsevier

GOTTMANN, J. (1961), *Megalopolis. The Urbanized Northeastern Seaboard of the United States*, MIT Press

GOULD, P. R. (1960), 'The development of the transportation pattern in Ghana', *Northwestern University Studies in Geography*, no. 5

GOULD, P. R. (1963), 'Man against his environment: a game-theoretic framework', *Annals*, Association of American Geographers, vol. 53, pp. 290–7

GOULD, P., and R. WHITE (1974), *Mental Maps*, Penguin

GOUROU, P. (1966), *The Tropical World*, 4th edition, Longman

GRANGER, C. W. J., and C. M. ELLIOTT (1967), 'A fresh look at wheat prices and markets in the eighteenth century', *Economic History Review*, vol. 20, pp. 257–65

GRIFFIN, E. (1973), 'Testing the von Thünen theory in Uruguay', *Geographical Review*, vol. 63, pp. 500–516

GRIGG, D. (1970), *The Harsh Lands. A Study in Agricultural Development*, Macmillan

GRIGG, D. B. (1974), *The Agricultural Systems of the World. An Evolutionary Approach*, Cambridge University Press

GRODINSKY, J. (1962), *Transcontinental Railway Strategy 1869–1893. A Study of Businessmen*, University of Pennsylvania Press

GUBSKY, N. (1921), 'The land settlement of Russia', *Economic Journal*, vol. 31, pp. 472–81

GÜSTEN, R. (1968), *Studies in the Staple Food Economy of Western Nigeria*, C. Hurst

HAGGETT, P., A. CLIFF, and A. FREY (1977), *Locational Analysis in Human Geography*, Arnold

HALL, P. (1966), *see* von Thünen (1826)

HAMILTON, F. E. I. (1974), 'A view of spatial behaviour, industrial organizations and decision-making', in F. E. I. Hamilton (ed.), *Spatial Perspectives on Industrial Organization and Decision-making*, Wiley, pp. 3–43

HAMMOND, N. (1974), 'Preclassic to Postclassic in northern Belize', *Antiquity*, vol. 48, pp. 177–89

HANCE, W. A. (1958), *African Economic Development*, Harper & Row

HARBISON, R. W. (1970), 'Colombia', in W. A. Lewis (ed.) *Tropical Development 1880–1913: Studies in Economic Progress*, Allen & Unwin, pp. 64–99

HARRIS, A. (1961), *The Rural Landscape of the East Riding of Yorkshire, 1700–1850*, Oxford University Press

HARRIS, R. C. (1966), *The Seigneurial System in Early Canada: a Geographical Study*, University of Wisconsin Press

HARRISON, A. J. (1963), 'Economies of scale and the structure of the road haulage industry', *Oxford Economic Papers*, vol. 15, pp. 287–307

HARVEY, D. W. (1963), 'Locational change in the Kentish hop industry and the analysis of land use patterns', *Transactions and Papers*, Institute of British Geographers, vol. 33, pp. 123–44

HAWKE, G. R. (1970), *Railways and Economic Growth in England and Wales, 1840–1870*, Clarendon Press

HAY, A. (1977), 'Some alternatives in the economic analysis of periodic marketing', *Geographical Analysis*, vol. 9, pp. 72–9

HEALY, K. T. (1940), *The Economics of Transportation in America*, Ronald Press

HELLEN, J. A. (1968), 'Rural economic development in Zambia, 1890–1964', *Afrika-Studien*, number 32, Weltforum Verlag

HEWES, L. (1973), *The Suitcase Farming Frontier*, University of Nebraska Press

HINTON, W. L. (1971), 'The economics of carrot production and marketing in Britain', *Occasional Papers*, no. 14, Department of Land Economy, University of Cambridge

HIRSCH, G. P. (1958), 'The size of farm holdings in England and Wales', *Farm Economist*, vol. 9, pp. 84–8

HIRST, M. A. (1970), 'Rural settlement and land use: a note on Tanzania', *Professional Geographer*, vol. 5, pp. 258–9

HIRST, M. A. (1978), 'Recent villagization in Tanzania', *Geography*, vol. 63, pp. 122–5

HODDER, B. W., and U. I. UKWU (1969), *Markets in West Africa*, Ibadan University Press

HODDER, I. (1977), 'Spatial studies in archaeology', *Progress in Geography*, vol. 1, pp. 33–64

HOFSTEE, E. W. (1957), *Rural Life and Rural Welfare in the Netherlands*, Government Printing and Publishing Office, The Hague (also private communication)

HOLZNER, L. (1970), 'The role of history and tradition in the urban geography of West Germany', *Annals*, Association of American Geographers, vol. 60, pp. 315–39

HOOVER, E. M. (1948), *The Location of Economic Activity*, McGraw-Hill

HORVATH, R. J. (1967), 'Von Thünen and urban sprawl', *Annals*, Association of American Geographers, vol. 57, pp. 811–12

HOSKINS, W. G. (1955), *The Making of the English Landscape*, Hodder & Stoughton

HOYLE, B. S. (ed.) (1973), *Transport and Development*, Macmillan

HUNT, E. H. (1973), *Regional Wage Variations in Britain 1850–1914*, Clarendon Press

HURWITZ, N. (1957), *Agriculture in Natal 1860–1950*, Oxford University Press

INTERNATIONAL BANK FOR RECONSTRUCTION AND DEVELOPMENT (1975), *Rural Electrification*, IBRD

JACKMAN, W. T. (1916), *The Development of Transportation in Modern England*, vol. 2, Cambridge University Press

JACKSON, R. T. (1970), 'Some observations on the von Thünen method of analysis with reference to southern Ethiopia', *East African Geographical Review*, vol. 8, pp. 39–46

JACKSON, R. T. (1971), 'Periodic markets in southern Ethiopia', *Transactions*, Institute of British Geographers, vol. 53, pp. 31–42

JACKSON, R. T. (1972), 'A vicious circle? – The consequences of von Thünen in tropical Africa', *Area*, vol. 4, pp. 258–61

JACOBY, E. H. (1959), *Land Consolidation in Europe*, International Institute for Land Reclamation and Improvement, Wageningen

JARMAN, M. R. (1972), 'A territorial model for archaeology: a behavioural and geographical approach', in D. L. Clarke (ed.), *Models in Archaeology*, Methuen, pp. 705–33

JOHNSON, B. F. (1958), *The Staple Food Economies of Western Tropical Africa*

JONASSON, O. (1925–6), 'Agricultural regions of Europe', *Economic Geography*, vol. 1, pp. 277–314; vol. 2, pp. 19–48

JONES, P. (1966), 'Medieval agrarian society in its prime: Italy', in M. M. Postan (ed.), *The Cambridge Economic History of Europe*, vol. 1, Cambridge University Press, pp. 340–431

JONES, R. C. (1976), 'Testing macro-Thünen models by linear programming', *Professional Geographer*, vol. 28, pp. 353–61

JONES, W. O. (1972), *Marketing Staple Food Crops in Tropical Africa*, Cornell University Press

JORDAN, T. G. (1974), 'Antecedents of the long-lot in Texas', *Annals*, Association of American Geographers, vol. 64, pp. 70–86

JOSHI, T. M., N. ANJANAIAH, and S. V. BHENDE (1968), *Studies in the Taxation of Agricultural Land and Income in India*, Asia Publishing House

JUMPER, S. R. (1969), 'The fresh vegetable industry in the USA. An example of dynamic interregional dependency', *Tijdschrift voor Economische en Sociale Geografie*, vol. 60, pp. 308–18

JUMPER, S. R. (1974), 'Wholesale marketing of fresh vegetables', *Annals*, Association of American Geographers, vol. 64, pp. 387–96

KAMPP, A. H. (1975), *An Agricultural Geography of Denmark*, Akadémia Kiadó

KARMON, Y. (1966), 'A geography of settlement in Eastern Nigeria', *Studies in Geography*, The Hebrew University, Jerusalem

KAYSER, B., and J. TRICART (1957), 'Rail et route au Sénégal', *Annales de Géographie*, vol. 66, pp. 328–50

KENNEDY, T. F. (1958), 'Village settlement in Tonga', *New Zealand Geographer*, vol. 14, pp. 161–72

KHAN, R. N. (1955), *Survey of Small Holdings in the Punjab*, Board of Economic Enquiry, Punjab (Pakistan)

KING, R. (1973), *Land Reform: the Italian Experience*, Butterworth
KIRK, J. H., and P. G. ELLIS (1971), *The United Kingdom Trade in Imported Fresh Fruit*, Wye College
KOEBNER, R. (1966), 'The settlement and colonization of Europe', in M. M. Postan (ed.), *The Cambridge Economic History of Europe*, vol. 1, Cambridge University Press, pp. 1–91
KOLLMORGAN, W. M., and G. F. JENKS (1958), 'Suitcase farming in Sully County, North Dakota', and 'Sidewalk farming in Toole County, Montana and Trail County, North Dakota', *Annals*, Association of American Geographers, vol. 48, pp. 27–40 and 209–31

LAHUEC, J.-P. (1970), 'Une communauté évolutive mossi Zaougho (Haute-Volta)', *Études Rurales*, vols. 37–38–39, pp. 151–72
LAMBERT, A. M. (1971), *The Making of the Dutch Landscape*, Seminar Press
LE LANNOU, M. (1941), *Pâtres et paysans de la Sardaigne*, Arrault
LARDNER, D. (1855), *Railway Economy: A Treatise on the New Art of Transport*; first published 1850; 1855 edition published by Harper & Brothers; reprinted 1968 by Augustus M. Kelley/David & Charles
LARSSON, G. (1947), *Inflyandet ar Auståndet från Bruckningscentrum till Inagojorden på Arbetsbehov, Driftsformer och Driftsresultat (The Influence of the Distance between the Farm Centre and the Farm Land upon the Need of Work, the Kind of Farming and the Economical Result*, with a summary in English)
DE LAVELEYE, E. (1901), *De la propriété et ses formes primitives*, 5th edition, Félix Alcan
LEAMAN, J. H., and E. C. CONKLING (1975), 'Transport change and agricultural specialization', *Annals*, Association of American Geographers, vol. 65, pp. 425–32
LEE, D. R., and G. T. SALLEE (1974), 'Theoretical patterns of farm shape and central place location', *Journal of Regional Science*, vol. 14, pp. 423–30
LEISTER, I. (1976), 'Peasant openfield farming and its territorial organization in County Tipperary', *Marburger Geographische Schriften*, vol. 69
LENNARD, R. (1959), *Rural England, 1086–1135: a Study of Agrarian Conditions*, Clarendon Press
LERICOLLAIS, A. (1970), 'La détérioration d'un terroir Sob, en

pays Sérèr (Sénégal)', *Études Rurales*, vols. 37–38–39, pp. 113–28

LESNE, M. (1962), 'Une expérience de déplacement de population: les centres de regroupement en Algérie', *Annales de Géographie*, vol. 71, pp. 567–603

LIPSEY, R. G. (1975), *An Introduction to Positive Economics*, 4th edition, Weidenfeld & Nicolson

LIPTON, M. (1968), 'The theory of the optimising peasant', *Journal of Development Studies*, vol. 4, pp. 327–51

LLOBET, S. (1958), 'Utilización del suelo y economía del agua en la región semiarida de Huercal-Overa (Almeria)', *Estudios Geográficos*, vol. 70, pp. 5–21

LOCKWOOD, B. (1971), *Samoan Village Economy*, Oxford University Press

LÖSCH, A. (1954), *The Economics of Location*, Yale University Press (translated from the German by W. H. Woglom)

LUDWIG, H.-D. (1968), 'Permanent farming on Ukara', in H. Ruthenberg (ed.), 'Smallholder farming and smallholder development in Tanzania', *Afrika-Studien*, vol. 24, pp. 87–135

MCCOURT, D. (1958), 'Surviving openfield in county Londonderry', *Ulster Folklife*, vol. 4, pp. 19–28

MACKINTOSH, W. A. (1934), *Prairie Settlement: The Geographical Setting*, Macmillan Company of Canada

MANSFIELD, E. (1965), 'Innovation and technical change in the railroad industry', in National Bureau of Economic Research, *Transportation Economics*, Columbia University Press, pp. 169–97

MANSHARD, W. (1975), 'Geography and environmental science', *Area*, vol. 7, pp. 147–55

MARCIANI, G. E. (1966), *L'Esperienza di Riforma Agraria in Italia*

MARTIN, H. (1956), *The Oil Palm Economy of the Ibibio Farmer*, Ibadan University Press

MAYHEW, A. (1971), 'Agrarian reform in West Germany. An assessment of the integrated development project Moorriem', *Transactions and Papers*, Institute of British Geographers, vol. 52, pp. 61–76

MEAD, W. R. (1953), *Farming in Finland*, Athlone Press

MEER, P. V. (1975), 'Land consolidation through land fragmentation: case studies from Taiwan', *Land Economics*, vol. 51, pp. 275–83

MEYNIER, A. (1958), *Les Paysages agraires*, Armand Colin

MINISTRY OF AGRICULTURE, FISHERIES AND FOOD (1967), *Horticulture in Britain, Part 1, Vegetables*, HMSO

MINISTRY OF AGRICULTURE, FISHERIES AND FOOD (1970), *Horticulture in Britain, Part 2, Fruit and Flowers*, HMSO

MIRACLE, M. P. (1967), *Agriculture in the Congo Basin*, University of Wisconsin Press

MORELAND, W. H. (1912), *The Agriculture of the United Provinces: an Introduction for the Use of Landholders and Officials*, 2nd edition, Government Press, Allahabad

MORGAN, W. B. (1955), 'Farming practice, settlement pattern and population density in south-eastern Nigeria', *Geographical Journal*, vol. 71, pp. 320–33

MORGAN, W. B. (1969), 'The zoning of land use around rural settlements in Tropical Africa', in M. F. Thomas and G. W. Whittington (eds.), *Environment and Land Use in Africa*, pp. 301–19, Methuen

MORGAN, W. B. (1973), 'The doctrine of the rings', *Geography*, vol. 58, pp. 301–12

MORTIMORE, M. J., and J. WILSON (1965), *Land and People in the Kano Close-Settled Zone*, Department of Geography, Ahmadu Bello University

MUKERJI, A. B. (1976), 'Rural settlements in the Chandigarh Siwalik Hills (India): a morphogenetic analysis', *Geografiska Annaler*, Series B, vol. 58, pp. 95–115

MULLER, P. O. (1973), 'Trend surfaces of American agricultural patterns: a macro-Thünian analysis', *Economic Geography*, vol. 49, pp. 228–42

MÜLLER-WILLE, W. (1936), *Die Ackerflüren in Landesteil Birkenfeld*, dissertation, University of Bonn. His map is reproduced in Lösch 1954, 382

MUNTON, R. J. (1974), 'Farming on the urban fringe', in J. H. Johnson (ed.), *Suburban Growth: Geographical Processes at the Edge of the Western City*, Wiley, pp. 201–23

NEALE, W. C. (1962), *Economic Change in Rural India: Land Tenure and Reform in Uttar Pradesh, 1800–1955*, Yale University Press

NELSON, M. (1973), *The Development of Tropical Lands: Policy Issues in Latin America*, Johns Hopkins Press

NEWIGER, N. (1968), 'Village settlement schemes', in H. Ruthenberg (ed.), 'Smallholder Farming and Smallholder Development in Tanzania', *Afrika-Studien*, vol. 24, pp. 249–73

NICOLAI, H., and J. JAQUES (1954), 'La transformation des paysages congolais par le chemin de fer. L'example du BCK', *Mémoires*, Institut Royal Colonial Belge, Section des Sciences Naturelles et Médicales, pp. 7–208

NIETSCHMANN, B. (1973), *Between Land and Water. The Subsistence Ecology of the Miskito Indians, Eastern Nicaragua*, Seminar Press

NORMAN, D. W. (1973), 'Economic analysis of agricultural production and labour utilization among the Hausu in the north of Nigeria', *African Rural Employment Paper*, no. 4, Michigan State University

ÖDMANN, E., and G. B. DAHLBERG (1970), *Urbanization in Sweden: Means and Methods for Planning*, Government Publishing House, Sweden

OHLIN, B. (1933), *Interregional and International Trade*, Harvard University Press, revised edition 1967

ÖHRLING, S. (1977), *Rural Change and Spatial Reorganization in Sri Lanka*, Curzon Press

OJO, G. J. A. (1973), 'Journey to agricultural work in Yorubaland', *Annals*, Association of American Geographers, vol. 63, pp. 85–96

OKALI, C. (1975), *Dominase. A Mobile Cocoa Farming Community in Brong-Ahafo*, Institute of Statistical, Social and Economic Research, University of Ghana

OLOYA, J. J., and T. T. POLEMAN (1969), *The Food Supply of Kampala*, Makerere Institute of Social Research

OLUWASANMI, H. A. (1967), 'The agricultural environment', in P. C. Lloyd *et al.* (eds.), *The City of Ibadan*, Cambridge University Press, pp. 27–33

OOI, J.-B. (1963), *Land, People and Economy in Malaya*, Longman

VON OPPENFIELD, H., J. VON OPPENFIELD, J. C. ST IGLESIA, and P. R. SANDOVAL (1957), *Farm Management, Land Use and Tenancy in the Philippines*, Central Experiment Station, Bulletin, no. 1

ORWIN, C. S., (1954), *The Open Fields*, 2nd edition, Clarendon Press

OWEN, W. (1968), *Distance and Development: Transport and Communications in India*, The Brookings Institution

PAGET, E. (1961), 'Value, valuation and use of land in the West Indies', *Geographical Journal*, vol. 127, pp. 493–8

PALLOT, J. (1977), 'Some preliminary thoughts on Soviet rural settlement planning', *Working Paper*, no. 206, Department of Geography, University of Leeds

PARRY, J. H. (1967), 'Transport and trade routes', in E. E. Rich and C. H. Wilson (eds.), *The Cambridge Economic History of Europe*, vol. 4, Cambridge University Press, pp. 155–219

PARSONS, J. J. (1957), 'Bananas in Ecuador: a new chapter in the history of tropical agriculture', *Economic Geography*, vol. 33, pp. 201–16

PATMORE, J. A. (1966), 'The contraction of the network of railway passenger services in England and Wales, 1836–1962', *Transactions*, Institute of British Geographers, vol. 38, pp. 105–18

PEET, J. R. (1969), 'The spatial expansion of commercial agriculture in the nineteenth century: a von Thünen interpretation', *Economic Geography*, vol. 45, pp. 283–301

PEET, J. R. (1970–71), 'von Thünen theory and the dynamics of agricultural expansion', *Explorations in Economic History*, vol. 8, pp. 181–201

PEET, J. R. (1972), 'Influences of the British market on agriculture and related economic development in Europe before 1860', *Transactions and Papers*, Institute of British Geographers, vol. 56, pp. 1–20

PELZER, K. J. (1945), *Pioneer Settlement in the Asiatic Tropics*, American Geographical Society

PHLIPPONNEAU, M. (1956), *La Vie rurale de la banlieue parisienne*, Armand Colin

PIEL-DESRUISSEAUX, J. (n.d.), *Cours d'organisation scientifique du travail en agriculture*, Institut d'Organisation Scientifique du Travail en Agriculture (mimeographed lecture notes)

PIHKALA, K. U., and S. SUOMELA (1952), 'Land fragmentation and measures of consolidation in Finland', *International Journal of Agrarian Affairs*, vol. 1, pp. 15–23

DE PLANHOL, X. (1961), *Nouveaux villages algérois*, Presses Universitaires de France

PONS, B. B. (1956), 'Evolución de la estructura agraria del Termino de Ocaña', *Estudios Geográficos*, vol. 63, pp. 185–206

POSTAN, M. (1952), 'The trade of medieval Europe: the north', in M. Postan and E. E. Rich (eds.), *The Cambridge Economic History of Europe*, vol. 2, Cambridge University Press, pp. 119–256

PRED, A. (1967 and 1969), 'Behavior and location: foundations for a geographic and dynamic location theory', *Lund Studies in Geography*, Series B, nos. 27 and 28

PRESTIANNI, N. (1947), *L'Economia Agraria delle Sicilia*

PRESTON, D. A. (1965), 'Changes in the economic geography of banana production in Ecuador', *Transactions and Papers*, Institute of British Geographers, vol. 37, pp. 77–90

PRESTON, D. A. (1974), 'Geographers among the peasants: research on rural societies in Latin America', in C. Board *et al.* (eds.), *Progress in Geography*, vol. 6, Arnold, pp. 143–78

PRICE, O. T. W. (1953), 'The economic significance of land as a factor of production, with particular reference to agricultural land', *Farm Economist*, vol. 7, pp. 239–53

PRINCE, H. (1971), 'Real, imagined and abstract worlds of the past', in C. Board *et al.* (eds.), *Progress in Geography*, vol. 3, Arnold, pp. 1–86

PROTHERO, R. M. (1957), 'Land use at Soba, Zaria Province, Northern Nigeria', *Economic Geography*, vol. 33, pp. 72–86

PRUNTY, M. C., and C. S. AIKEN (1972), 'The demise of the Piedmont cotton region', *Annals*, Association of American Geographers, vol. 62, pp. 283–306

RAYNER, A. J. (1975), 'Regional price differentiation policies for milk in England and Wales: an empirical evaluation using a spatial equilibrium framework', *Bulletin*, no. 149, Department of Agricultural Economics, University of Manchester

RAZSO, I. (1959), *Agricultural Mechanization. The General Problem of Transport on the Farm*, United Nations, Economic Commission for Europe

REINIG, C. C. (1970), 'Zande subsistence and food production', in P. F. M. McLoughlin (ed.), *African Food Production Systems*, Johns Hopkins Press, pp. 125–63

REPUBLIC OF KENYA (1966), *Report of the Mission on Land Consolidation and Registration in Kenya 1965–1966*

RICHARDS, A. I. (1958), 'A changing pattern of agriculture in East Africa: the Bemba of Northern Rhodesia', *Geographical Journal*, vol. 124, pp. 302–14

RICHARDSON, B. C. (1974), 'Distance regularities in Guyanese rice cultivation', *Journal of Developing Areas*, vol. 8, pp. 235–55

ROCHEFORT, R. (1961), *Le Travail en Sicile. Étude de géographie sociale*, Presses Universitaires de France

ROLL, E. (1938), *A History of Economic Thought*, Faber & Faber

RUTHENBERG, H. (ed.) (1968), 'Smallholder farming and small-holder development in Tanzania', *Afrika-Studien*, vol. 24

SALISBURY, R. F. (1970), *Vunamami. Economic Transformation in a Traditional Society*, University of California Press

SAMUELSON, P. A. (1976), *Economics*, 10th edition, McGraw-Hill

SANDHU, K. S. (1964), 'Emergency resettlement in Malaya', *Journal of Tropical Geography*, vol. 18, pp. 157–83

SAUTTER, G. (1962), 'À propos de quelques terroirs d'Afrique occidentale: essai comparatif', *Études Rurales*, vol. 4, pp. 24–86

SAUTTER, G. (1975), 'Une enquête exemplaire: l'emploi du temps agricole en pays Zandé,' *Études Rurales*, vol. 60, pp. 73–88

SAWYER, P. H. (1976), *Medieval Settlement: Continuity and Change*, Arnold

SCHLEBECKER, J. T. (1960), 'The world metropolis and the history of American agriculture', *Journal of Economic History*, vol. 20, pp. 187–208

DE SCHLIPPÉ, P. (1956), *Shifting Cultivation in Africa: the Zande system of agriculture*, Routledge & Kegan Paul

SCHULER, E. (1957), 'Untersuchungen über verbundene Flur-bereinigungs und Assiedlungsverfahren in Baden-Wurttemburg', *Schriftenreihe für Flurbereinigung*, West German Federal Ministry of Food, Agriculture and Forestry

SCHULTZ, T. W. (1951), 'The declining economic importance of agricultural land', *Economic Journal*, vol. 61, pp. 725–40

SCHULTZ, T. W. (1964), *Transforming Traditional Agriculture*, Yale University Press

SCOTT, P. (1968), 'Population and land use in Australia', *Tijdschrift voor Economische en Sociale Geografie*, vol. 59, pp. 237–44

SEN, L. K. et al. (1971), *Planning Rural Growth Centres for Integrated Area Development. A Study of Miryalguda Taluka*, National Institute of Community Development, Hyderabad

SINCLAIR, R. (1967), 'Von Thünen and urban sprawl', *Annals*, Association of American Geographers, vol. 57, pp. 72–87

SKOVGARD, K. (1953), 'Consolidation of agricultural land in Denmark', in B. O. Binni (ed.), *The Consolidation of Fragmented Agricultural Holdings*, FAO Agricultural Studies, no. 11, pp. 41–55

SKRUBBELTRANG, F. (1953), *Agricultural Development and Land Reform in Denmark*, FAO Agricultural Studies, no. 22, pp. 7–73

SLICHER VAN BATH, B. H. (1963), *The Agrarian History of Western Europe AD 500–1850*, Arnold (translation by O. Ordish)

DE SMET, R. E. (1972), 'Une enquête budget-temps dans les Uélé (République du Zaire)', in *Études de géographie tropicale offertes à Pierre Gourou*, Mouton, pp. 287–300

SMITH, C. T. (1967), *An Historical Geography of Western Europe before 1800*, Longman

SMITH, D. M. (1971), *Industrial Location: An Economic Geographical Analysis*, Wiley

SMITH, E. G. (1975), 'Fragmented farms in the United States', *Annals, Association of American Geographers*, vol. 65, pp. 58–70

SMITH, R. H. T. (1971), 'West African market places: temporal periodicity and locational spacing', in C. Meillassoux (ed.), *The Development of Indigenous Trade and Markets in West Africa*, Oxford University Press, pp. 319–46

SMITH, W. (1953), *An Economic Geography of Great Britain*, 2nd edition, Methuen

SOJA, E. W. (1968), *The Geography of Modernization in Kenya: A Spatial Analysis of Social, Economic, and Political Change*, Syracuse University Press

SORBI, U. (1955), *Borgo a Mozzano*

SORRENSON, M. P. K. (1967), *Land Reform in the Kikuyu Country. A Study in Government Policy*, Oxford University Press

SPENCER, J. E. (1966), 'Shifting cultivation in southeastern Asia', *University of California Publications in Geography*, no. 19, University of California Press

SPIEGEL, H. W. (1971), *The Growth of Economic Thought*, Prentice-Hall

STAMER, H. H. (1952), *Die Standortsorientierung der Landwirtschaft um den Grossmarkt Hamburg*, unpublished doctoral dissertation, Kiel

STEEL, R. W. (1947), 'Ashanti Survey, 1945–46: an experiment in social research', *Geographical Journal*, vol. 110, pp. 149–79

STURROCK, F. (1958), 'Designing cattle yards to save labour', *The Esso Farmer*, Summer, pp. 1–5

SUBLETT, M. D. (1975), 'Farmers on the road', *Research Paper*, no. 168, Department of Geography, University of Chicago

SUOMELA, S. (1950), 'Peltojen Sijainnin Vaikutuksesta Maatilan Talouteen', *Acta Agralia Fennica*, vol. 71 ('On the influence of the location of fields on farming', with a summary in English).

There is a brief summary in the *International Journal of Agrarian Affairs*, 1952, pp. 18–22

SUTTON, K. (1977), 'Rural land development and resettlement in Sabah, Malaysia', *Pacific Viewpoint*, May, pp. 79–92

SVIMEZ (1950), *Informazióni SVIMEZ*, April, pp. 12–19 and 221–4

SYMONS, L. and C. WHITE (1975), *Russian Transport. An Historical and Geographical Survey*, Bell

TAKES, A. P. (1958), *Physical Planning in Connection with Land Reclamation and Improvement*, International Institute for Land Reclamation and Improvement, Wageningen

TAKES, A. P. (1975), *Land Settlement and Resettlement Projects. Some Guidelines for Their Planning and Implementation*, International Institute for Land Reclamation and Improvement, Wageningen

TAYLOR, G. R. (1951), *The Transportation Revolution 1815–1860*, Rinehart

THIRSK, J. (ed.) (1967), *The Agrarian History of England and Wales, vol. 4, 1500–1640*, Cambridge University Press

THORPE, H. (1951), 'The influence of inclosure on the form and pattern of rural settlement in Denmark', *Transactions and Papers, Institute of British Geographers*, vol. 17, pp. 113–28

VON THÜNEN, J. H. (1826), *Der isolierte Staat in Beziehung auf Landswirtschaft und Nationalökonomie*, F. Perthes. An English translation appeared in 1966 as *Von Thünen's Isolated State*, edited by P. Hall, Pergamon

TIMMS, D. (1971), *The Urban Mosaic. Towards a Theory of Residential Differentiation*, Cambridge University Press

TINDITUUZA, R. J., and B. M. KATEETE (1971), 'Essays on land fragmentation in Kigezi District', *Occasional Paper*, no. 22, Department of Geography, Makerere University

TRAPNELL, C. G., and J. N. CLOTHIER (1936), *The Soils, Vegetation and Agricultural Systems of North Western Rhodesia*, Government Printer, Lusaka

TUAN, YI-FU (1977), *Space and Place: The Perspective of Experience*, Arnold

UNITED STATES DEPARTMENT OF AGRICULTURE (1953), *Regional Variations in Prices Received by Farmers*, USDA

UNITED STATES DEPARTMENT OF AGRICULTURE (1969), 'The

economics of farm products transportation', *Marketing Research Report*, no. 843, USDA

USHER, A. P. (1913), *The History of the Grain Trade in France, 1400–1700*, reissued in 1973 by Octagon Books

VAN VALKENBURG, S., and C. C. HELD (1952), *Europe*, Wiley

VIRRI, T. J. (1946), 'Maanjako-olojen Vaikutuksesta Maataloustuotantous', *Maatalous Agronomien Yhdistkysen Julkaisa*, pp. 6–11

VISSER, W. C. (1950), 'Gedachten en Getallen over de Geldelijke Gevolgen van Ruilverkalen', *Landbouwkundig Tijdschrift*, pp. 993–1010

VITA-FINZI, C., and E. S. HIGGS (1970), 'Prehistoric economy in the Mount Carmel area of Palestine: site catchment analysis', *Proceedings*, Prehistoric Society, vol. 36, pp. 1–37

VÖRÖSMARTI, E. T. (1976), 'Demographic characteristics of rural settlements', in Gy Enyedi (ed.), *Rural Transformation in Hungary*, Akadémia Kiadó, pp. 27–40

DE VRIES, J. (1974), *The Dutch Rural Economy in the Golden Age, 1500–1700*, Yale University Press

WAGENBUUR, H. T. M. (1972), 'Labour and development. An analysis of the time-budget and of production and productivity of lime farmers in southern Ghana', *Occasional Papers*, Institute of Social Studies, The Hague

WALD, H. P. (1959), *Taxation of Agricultural Lands in Underdeveloped Economies*, Harvard University Press

WALLERSTEIN, I. (1974), *The Modern World System. Capitalist Agriculture and the Origins of the European World-economy in the Sixteenth Century*, Academic Press

WANMALI, S. (1976), 'Popular participation and organisation, distribution and consumption of social services and facilities in rural human settlements: an Indian experience', unpublished typescript, Department of Geography, University of Cambridge

WARD, R. G. (1968), 'Reshaping New Guinea's geography', Inaugural Lecture, University of Papua New Guinea

WARNTZ, W. (1959), *Toward a Geography of Price*, University of Pennsylvania Press

WATSON, W. (1963), *North America: Its Countries and Regions*, Longman

WATTERS, R. F. (1971), *Shifting Cultivation in Latin America*, FAO

WATTS, H. D. (1974), 'Locational adjustment in the British beet sugar industry', *Geography*, vol. 59, pp. 10–23

WEBBER, M. J. (1972), *Impact of Uncertainty on Location*, MIT Press

WEBER, A. (1929), *Theory of the Location of Industries*, University of Chicago Press (English translation by C. J. Friedrich)

WEITZ, R., *et al.* (1971), *Uda-Walawe Project, Ceylon. A Comparative Study of Two Regional Planning Alternatives*, Settlement Study Centre, Rehovot, Israel

WELLINGTON, A. M. (1898), *The Economic Theory of the Location of Railways*, 6th edition

WEST, R. C., and J. P. AUGELLI (1966), *Middle America: Its Lands and Peoples*, Prentice-Hall

WHETHAM, E. H. (1964), 'The London milk trade, 1860–1900', *Economic History Review*, vol. 17, pp. 369–80

WHETHAM, E. H. (1970), *The London Milk Trade 1900–1930*, Institute of Agricultural History, University of Reading

WHETHAM, E. H. (1972), *Agricultural Marketing in Africa*, Oxford University Press

WHETSTONE, L. (1970), *The Marketing of Milk*, Research Monograph, Institute of Economic Affairs

WHETTEN, N. L. (1948), *Rural Mexico*, University of Chicago Press

WHITE, G. F. (1945), 'Human adjustment to floods: a geographical approach to the flood problem in the United States', *Research Paper*, no. 29, Department of Geography, University of Chicago

WHITE, G. F., *et al.* (1972), *Drawers of Water. Domestic Use of Water in East Africa*, University of Chicago Press

WIIALA, A. (1948), *Uusjaon Vaikutuksesta Jakokunnau Maatalousteen*

WIKKRAMATILEKE, R., and K. SINGH (1970), 'Tradition and change in an Indian dairying community in Singapore', *Annals*, Association of American Geographers, vol. 60, pp. 717–42

WILLAN, T. S. (1936), *River Navigation in England, 1600–1750*, Oxford University Press

WILLIAMS, M. (1972), 'The enclosure of waste land in Somerset, 1700–1900', *Transactions*, Institute of British Geographers, vol. 57, pp. 99–123

WILLS, J. B. (ed.) (1962), *Agriculture and Land Use in Ghana*, Oxford University Press

WILSON, G. W., *et al.* (1966), *The Impact of Highway Investment on Development*, The Brookings Institution

WOLFF, H. W. (1918), *The Future of our Agriculture*, P. S. King

WOLPERT, J. (1964), 'The decision process in spatial context', *Annals*, Association of American Geographers, vol. 54, pp. 537–58

YOKENO, N. (1956), 'Thünen's structure in the agriculture of Japan', *Sophia Economic Review*, vol. 3, pp. 14–22

DE YOUNG, J. E. (1955), *Village Life in Modern Thailand*, University of California Press

Index

Carole Naisbitt,